5:2 LIFESTYLE

more than 100 recipes plus
4 weeks of menu plans

DELPHINE DE MONTALIER
& CHARLOTTE DEBEUGNY

PHOTOGRAPHY BY CHARLOTTE LASCÈVE

MURDOCH BOOKS

CONTENTS

Delphine de Montalier and Charlotte Debeugny have been passionate about healthy and balanced eating for a long time. The aim of this book is to adapt the 5:2 diet to French cuisine, which has a rich gourmet heritage, by using fresh and delicious ingredients in new, creative ways.

Their unique concept is the 'Super 500'

This is a dish that contains the maximum amount of vitamins and minerals while obeying the rule of only 500 or 600 calories (2092 or 2510 kilojoules) on the two weekly Fast Days. These meals reduce the time spent in the kitchen, as you only need to cook once during the day. They can be prepared the day before and they're portable, so you can enjoy them at work or when you're on the move. Lastly, they offer the perfect balance of protein, carbohydrates and vegetables to ensure you're full of health and vitality. With energy and a positive outlook you'll get through the Fast Days without too much difficulty, if any!

5:2 COACHING

Can you really lose weight by dieting only two days per week?

'Intermittent fasting' is the latest trend in dieting. Originating in the UK, it has spread around the world. Based on solid research, its effectiveness has been scientifically proven, unlike many fashionable diets.

The basic principle is to eat less, which allows you to lose weight and offers numerous health benefits.

The advantage of this method? Flexibility!

You don't need to eat less every day, only on certain days. These are the Fast Days. There should be at least two Fast Days per week. It's referred to as the 5:2 diet, because each week you have two days of restricted eating and five 'normal' days, the Non-Fast Days. After a month of intermittent fasting, or only nine days of restricted caloric intake, weight loss can reach up to 3 kg (almost 7 lb), or even more. So why not try it? Many people focus on what they should eat on the Fast Days. The advice is to eat no more than 25% of the usual recommended calorie intake, which comes to about 500 calories (2092 kilojoules) for women and 600 calories (2510 kilojoules) for men. But it's also important to consider what should be eaten on the other five days.

Can you really eat absolutely anything, including hamburgers, chips and unlimited chocolate cake?

Of course, you can have dessert and drink alcohol on the Non-Fast Days if you like. But eating like a sparrow for two days and then gorging on junk food on the other five is far from healthy, even if you obey the rules of intermittent fasting! The aim is to make balanced and tasty meals on the Non-Fast Days just as you do on the Fast Days, so you feel in good shape and stay that way.

Why should you eat less?

Studies on animals have shown that a reduction in calorie intake leads to weight loss, improved physical condition and longer life expectancy. However, it can be difficult to subject yourself to a limited calorie intake on a permanent basis. This is why scientists have begun to examine the effectiveness of restricting calories on a limited number of days, allowing the animals to eat their fill on other days. This method has proved to be effective: alternating fasting days and days of 'normal' eating had the same effect as a permanent restriction on the number of calories.

This data forms the basis of the theory of intermittent fasting.[1] The first human studies[2] are recent and, each time, intermittent fasting has had a positive effect on health markers such as weight, cholesterol, blood pressure and blood sugar levels. Long-term trials are underway to evaluate the effectiveness of calorie restriction on people who do not suffer from obesity.

How to use this book

1 Reread the advice about the diet.

2 Prepare your meals with the help of the suggested recipes.

3 Eventually follow the one-month program suggested at the end of the book: one month of menu plans based on the principles of intermittent fasting, alternating Fast-Day recipes and suggestions for healthy and balanced meals on the other five days. We are convinced it is possible to create and enjoy delicious and easy seasonal menus, and enhance your health and vitality at the same time.

.... *Did you know?* ....

Some say that intermittent fasting reproduces the way we ate in prehistoric times, with periods of abundance and other times when food was rationed. In many cultures, periods of fasting are practised for spiritual reasons, but also for reasons of physical health.

1 JE Brown, M Mosley and S Aldred, 'Intermittent fasting: a dietary intervention for prevention of diabetes and cardiovascular disease?', *British Journal of Diabetes & Vascular Disease*, 13: 68, 2013.

2 Anton, S, 'Fasting or caloric restriction for Healthy Aging', *Christiaan Leeuwenburgh Experimental Gerontology*, vol. 48, no. 10: 1003–1005, October 2013.

THE PRINCIPLE
OF THE DIET

Our diet is structured over the course of a week. It includes two days when food intake shouldn't exceed 500 calories (2092 kilojoules) per day for women and 600 calories (2510 kilojoules) for men. These two days are called Fast Days. They aren't necessarily taken together. On the other five days, called the Non-Fast Days, the idea is to eat normally.

How does it work?

On two days each week (not necessarily in a row), calorie intake is reduced to 25% of the normal intake. To maintain a stable weight, a woman needs an average of 2000 calories (8368 kilojoules) per day and a man 2500 calories (10,460 kilojoules). So, on Fast Days, a woman should consume no more than 500 calories (2092 kilojoules) and a man 600 (2510 kilojoules). Why 25%? Numerous studies on total fasting (no food for 24 hours or more) or calorie restriction (eating less on a permanent basis) show that the 25% rule is the maximum amount of food that can be consumed without losing the benefits of fasting. This is the threshold at which studies on animals start to show positive effects on health. Then, on the Non-Fast Days, while you need to be sensible (don't overcompensate by going up to 150%!), you can satisfy your appetite without any problems.

A SIMPLE DIET
Studies show that many diets are difficult to follow because they require you to limit your calorie intake every day. This is why it is so difficult to lose weight in a sustainable way. With intermittent fasting, your intake is only limited on two days. On the other days, you can relax and enjoy tasty little dishes that are richer but still healthy and balanced.

A FLEXIBLE DIET
You can choose and plan your Fast Days according to your own schedule. They don't need to be together and you can even organise them at the last minute, in case your plans change.

A DIET THAT LETS YOU EAT
The 5:2 diet is not about eliminating certain food groups, eating diet foods or taking expensive dietary supplements. Over time, the meals on your Non-Fast Days will naturally become lower in fat and higher in vegetables and proteins. We believe that to get the full benefit from intermittent fasting, you should make healthy and balanced meals on your Non-Fast Days as well.

Speaking for ourselves, around 80% of the time we eat balanced meals, and the rest of the time we eat completely freely, for pleasure! Fatty and overly sugary foods don't often make it past the door of our homes and we allow ourselves to be more decadent during dinners with friends, celebrations and holidays. It's up to you to find the method and rhythm that suits you best so that the majority of your meals are healthy and high in essential nutrients.

A healthy diet is not an end in itself but a path to follow. It's just a target. The emphasis should be on health rather than on weight—studies show that people who adopt this attitude manage their weight better. Make a list of five reasons, apart from weight, why you'd like to try intermittent fasting and keep them within easy reach. So, what are they? More energy, a glowing complexion, a sharper mind. Your personalised list will help to keep you motivated.

THE BENEFITS
OF INTERMITTENT FASTING

The 5:2 diet promotes weight loss, but it's not the only positive effect. It improves your state of health on several levels.

Weight loss

One of the main motivations for intermittent fasting is weight loss.

1 Restricting intake to 500 calories (2092 kilojoules) for women and 600 calories (2510 kilojoules) for men two days a week (with a normal diet on the other five days) amounts to 3000–3800 fewer calories (12,552–15,910 kilojoules) per week. Considering that 1 kg (2 lb 4 oz) of fat has a calorific value of around 7000 (29,288 kilojoules), it is possible to lose half a kilo (just over 1 lb) per week. The good news is that many people lose even more weight. It's recommended that you practise intermittent fasting over an extended period of time, because it seems to encourage the body to burn fat even more efficiently. After a month, the average weight loss is around 3 kg (almost 7 lb) for women and up to 5 kg (a little over 11 lb) for men. In addition, intermittent fasting increases the production of a tiny gene called SIRT1, which helps accelerate weight loss by reducing fat storage and activating lipid metabolism.

2 Another effect of intermittent fasting is that the body gets accustomed to being satisfied with smaller portions, which allows us to become aware of what we really need to feed ourselves. You can also become an expert in calorie counting, which will be useful for Non-Fast Days.

3 Other people have told us that intermittent fasting enables them to experience a 'feeling of hunger' without feeling like they're starving and reacting immediately to their symptoms by eating. In the obesogenic environment we live in, food is omnipresent. Intermittent fasting conditions you to tolerate this feeling of hunger in the short term until the next meal.

4 Our concept of the 'Super 500' dishes means the body doesn't become nutrient-deficient while fasting. That way, the body doesn't compensate for it afterwards by storing richer foods.

Improved health markers

1 Studies on animals indicate that a reduction in calories leads to a slight tension in the cells and the body in general. This tension seems to help cells protect themselves against wear and tear. Intermittent fasting promotes a process called autophagy, which enables cells to repair themselves by themselves and eliminate any toxins more efficiently.

2 Research has shown that this process helps to reduce inflammation. Inflammation is connected to a number of medical conditions such as cerebral degeneration, type 2 diabetes, cardiovascular diseases, cancer and other age-related diseases. It seems that intermittent fasting reduces inflammatory markers, particularly by improving the way the body regulates its blood sugar levels, due to a better response of the cells to insulin.

3 Studies have shown that intermittent fasting helps to lower cholesterol levels.

If your goal is truly to optimise and improve some of these health markers, you should also pay attention to what you eat on the Non-Fast Days. Without going to the trouble of counting calories, you should try to eat as healthily as possible.

The fight against ageing

When people talk about the fight against ageing, we usually think of anti-wrinkle creams that are supposed to give you a radiant complexion, or even botox and cosmetic surgery. Without wanting to come across as prophets of doom, we also need to think about our brains and the risks of dementia and similar age-related diseases. Studies show that intermittent fasting tends to stimulate brain function and reduce the risk of injury or illness. It stimulates the production of protective factors that enhance neuronal function and helps the brain resist ageing and preserve its functions. According to studies on animals, it protects neurons against Alzheimer's, Parkinson's and Huntington's diseases, and against strokes.[3]

The most visible aspect of ageing is the skin. The older it gets, the more vulnerable it is to damage caused by internal or external toxins. Intermittent fasting helps cells to repair and renew themselves more quickly. It increases the production of a hormone called somatropin hormone (or STH), which helps strengthen skin functions, muscles, tendons, ligaments and bones. Somatropin also improves skin by reducing wrinkles and fine lines.

Who should not practise intermittent fasting?

Even though we fully support the principle of intermittent fasting, it is important to stress that this diet is not recommended for certain groups of people for various reasons:

- Children and adolescents.
- People suffering from diseases such as diabetes or other problems concerning the control of blood sugar levels.
- People suffering from digestive disorders such as irritable bowel syndrome, Crohn's disease or ulcerative colitis.
- People suffering from depression or chronic stress or who are naturally anxious.
- People who have shown signs of having an eating disorder.
- People taking certain medications, in particular diabetes medications or beta-blockers.
- Pregnant or breastfeeding women.
- Athletes and/or elite sportspeople.
- People suffering from obesity.

If in doubt, we recommend consulting your doctor. And even if you don't follow the dietary restrictions of Fast Days, you can still enjoy our delicious recipes and menu ideas for the five Non-Fast Days.

---

[3] MP Mattson, W Duan and Z Guo, 'Meal size and frequency affect neuronal plasticity and vulnerability to disease: cellular and molecular mechanisms', *Journal of Neurochemistry*, 84(3): 417–31, February 2003.

.... *Did you know?* ....

The body produces two hormones for regulating blood sugar levels. Blood sugar levels need to be strictly controlled because if they are abnormally high, the sugar can cause damage to the body's organs and cells. Insulin is a hormone that's released in response to high blood sugar levels. It helps move the sugar (glucose) from the bloodstream into the cells, where it is stored or used as energy. Glucagon, on the other hand, is a hormone released in response to low blood sugar levels. It helps move the sugar stored in the cells into the bloodstream.

Are you lost? Simply put: insulin promotes fat storage whereas glucagon helps to burn it. Intermittent fasting helps cells respond more efficiently to insulin, preventing it from being released in too large a quantity. Intermittent fasting, therefore, helps you to burn fat!

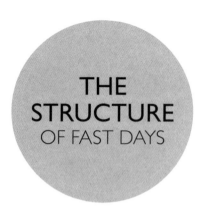

THE STRUCTURE
OF FAST DAYS

On the Fast Days calorie intake is restricted, but these days are nothing to worry about. By learning to understand different foods and what they give you, you'll sail through these days.

When should I eat?

The advantage of intermittent fasting is that you can structure your Fast Days to suit you. You can choose to have breakfast, then a snack at noon and a light dinner, or skip a meal and divide the calories between lunch and dinner, or breakfast and dinner. You can also try to have only one meal a day, but we'd advise you not to attempt this option until you get used to intermittent fasting.

Our menu suggestions for Fast Days are based on two meals a day, lunch and dinner, for the following reasons:

- Breakfast tends to stimulate your appetite (it does ours anyway!).
- Breakfast is probably the easiest meal to skip.
- The fasting period is naturally extended, so you can burn a greater amount of fat. If you finish dinner at around 9 pm the night before and don't eat before 1 pm the next day, this amounts to a 16-hour fast.

Is it really healthy to skip breakfast?

Past studies have shown that people who eat breakfast tend to have healthier eating habits (exercising more, eating more vegetables and less sugar) than those who skip breakfast. Though it has been recommended in the past to 'never skip breakfast', we have learned that it is not necessarily the fact of eating breakfast that guarantees better health. Eating breakfast does not kickstart metabolism or give any extra health benefits on its own.

Do the two Fast Days need to be together?

The two Fast Days don't necessarily have to be together. We recommend (for the more adventurous) practising intermittent fasting on two non-consecutive days for the first two weeks, then two consecutive days for the last two weeks. The difference is not necessarily noticeable in terms of weight loss, but it means the Fast Days are over with sooner. Some people actually find it easier to keep going with their fasting once they've started. Their body needs to get used to fasting. This is difficult for some, but after three to four days, the body gets used to experiencing hunger without insisting on food. It's possible to live with the feeling of hunger with no problem. After a few weeks of practice, it's no longer a hardship. It's a way of life!

.... What are calories .... and kilojoules?

Calories and kilojoules are measures of the energy in food and drinks. One calorie equals about 4.2 kilojoules. We use these to supply energy to our body, or to store the energy for later use. The calories/kilojoules in the different food groups and alcohol are counted in the following way:

1 g fat = 9 cal/38 kJ
1 g protein = 4 cal/17 kJ
1 g carbohydrate = 4 cal/17 kJ
1 g of alcohol = 7 cal/29 kJ

The foods that are richest in calories/kilojoules are fats, followed by alcohol!

What should I eat?

QUALITY AND QUANTITY

On the Fast Days, every calorie counts. You really need to be conscious of the quantities of food you consume. We recommend eating good quality food on these days. You can, of course, use up your recommended calories by eating a few squares of chocolate, but that will not give you the nutrients you need to help manage your hunger. To manage your Fast Days easily, we suggest you balance your meals with protein, unrefined carbohydrates and lots of vegetables.

PROTEINS

Protein-rich foods have a low glycaemic index[4], and are therefore digested slowly, helping you feel full. It is essential to eat protein in sufficient quantities on Fast Days. Foods that are high in protein and low in calories include white fish, crustaceans, eggs and poultry. Pulses in small quantities are also a good source of protein and contain little fat.

STARCHES

Starchy foods (grains, potatoes, rice, pasta …) are high in carbohydrates. Most importantly, we recommend whole grains, which contain more fibre than refined (white) grains and have a lower glycaemic load (GL). They are a good source of sustainable energy.

FRUITS AND VEGETABLES

Vegetables are generally low in calories and can be eaten in large quantities to fill out meals. They provide lots of vitamins and minerals as well as fibre, which means they're digested more slowly. Their energy is, therefore, released in a measured way. Fruits contain more calories: you can eat them on Fast Days, but pay attention to quantities.

FATS

We don't have anything against 'good' fats, which are essential for many bodily processes and functions. According to research, we should eat more omega-3 fatty acids (found in oily fish, nuts and seeds) and mono-unsaturated fatty acids (found in olive oil and avocado). These fats can be easily incorporated into meals on the five Non-Fast Days, but should only be eaten in very small amounts on the Fast Days. A teaspoon of vegetable oil, for example, represents about 45 calories (188 kilojoules) and 15 g (1/2 oz) of nuts 'costs' 100 calories (418 kilojoules)!

BEVERAGES

We suggest you avoid drinking any alcohol on Fast Days to give your liver a rest. Alcohol is a source of empty calories, and the goal is to optimise your intake of nutrients on fasting days.

[4] The glycaemic index measures how quickly foods are digested. A low index indicates that the food will be digested slowly.

A 125 ml (4 fl oz/1/2 cup) glass of wine contains about 90 calories (377 kilojoules). A small can of beer contains about 155 calories (649 kilojoules). Save those calories for Non-Fast Days instead. You can drink as much water, tea and herbal tea as you like on Fast Days (without sugar or milk). We recommend limiting caffeine to no more than four cups of coffee per day. People tend to drink more coffee on Fast Days to ease their hunger and compensate for their lack of energy—but be aware that caffeine has a stronger effect on people with an empty stomach, causing palpitations or other symptoms in sensitive individuals. We also advise against diet drinks, which contain artificial ingredients. Water remains the cheapest and healthiest drink! Why not flavour your water naturally with mint leaves, lemon verbena or lemon slices?

FLAVOURFUL MEALS

In our recipes, we use low-calorie but flavour-packed ingredients such as fresh herbs, citrus zest and spices, because flavourful meals help you enjoy Fast Days. We give preference to cooking methods that preserve the most vitamins and minerals.

calorie (kilojoule) table

100 CALORIES (418 KILOJOULES) of raw proteins	100 CALORIES (418 KILOJOULES) of raw grains	100 CALORIES (418 KILOJOULES) of raw fruits and vegetables
100 g (3½ oz) chicken breast fillet	30 g (1 oz) rice	700 g (1 lb 9 oz) green leafy vegetables
60 g (2¼ oz) lean beef	25 g (1 oz) quinoa	200 g (7 oz) carrots
120 g (4¼ oz) white fish	40 g (1½ oz) bread	500 g (1 lb 2 oz) cherry tomatoes
30 g (1 oz) lentils	25 g (1 oz) pasta	1 medium banana
15 g (½ oz) almonds	30 g (1 oz) rice vermicelli	200 g (7 oz) berries

Examples of combinations for Fast Days with two meals:
Meal 1 = 100 g (3½ oz) chicken + 30 g (1 oz) rice + 1 enormous salad
Meal 2 = 25 g (1 oz) quinoa + mixed vegetables + 15 g (½ oz) walnuts

tips for Fast Days

One day or another, you'll have trouble fasting.

Simply swap days and postpone your fast until later. It's easier to fast on a day when you're working or busy than a day spent at home or with the family. We found that Mondays and Thursdays were the best days for us.

Try to think about other things besides food on fasting days.

Above all, don't spend the whole day thinking about what you're going to eat the next day! Make the most of both the Fast Days and the Non-Fast Days.

The first week of intermittent fasting is often the hardest.

The second week will already be easier. Choose your days wisely in the first week and make sure you're busy on these days.

Plan your meals.

- Try to eat healthy, nourishing, enjoyable food with maximum nutritional value so you feel satisfied. Give priority to proteins, vegetables and unrefined grains.
- Avoid empty calories. Alcohol and highly processed or sugary foods are low in nutrients and fibre, and the body absorbs them too quickly. Therefore, you feel hungry again sooner.
- Avoid ready-to-eat pre-cooked meals, especially diet meals, which often hide a lot of refined carbohydrates and salt. Instead, try our everyday and practical 'Super 500' recipes!
- Eat fresh foods. Because each calorie counts, use them in fresh, appetising and flavourful meals instead of pre-cooked meals, meal replacements or high-protein drinks.
- However, if you really do not have the time or inclination to cook, buy a packet of pre-cooked rice, a few prawns or chickpeas and salad—a real gourmet 'Fast' meal (you can find all the calorie information on the packets).

Stay hydrated.

This is an important point. In effect, since your food intake is limited on Fast Days, the amount of water provided by food is also reduced. Your body can also confuse hunger and thirst. Drink a glass of water with each meal and whenever you feel hunger coming on.

Find the right rhythm.

One of the advantages of intermittent fasting is its flexibility, so make the most of it.

Do you have trouble getting to sleep at night on Fast Days?

We found that the combination of protein and vegetables at dinner time could disturb sleep. This problem seems to be solved by adding a small amount of unrefined carbohydrates (brown rice or quinoa). In effect, carbohydrates stimulate the absorption of certain proteins that are used to make serotonin, a neurotransmitter that helps promote the sleep cycle.

At the start, weigh the ingredients until you have a better idea of portion sizes.

Are you hungry?

- Try drinking a glass of water and waiting 20 minutes. Your body can sometimes confuse hunger and thirst.
- Distract yourself: take a walk, go back to your work, chat with a friend, read a magazine.
- Learn how to recognise hunger and tell yourself it will eventually pass. You won't die of hunger from waiting an hour or two before eating.
- Allow yourself a little snack—for example, 15 g (½ oz) raw nuts or a punnet of fresh berries. You can then either adjust the other meals to take the snack into account or have a fasting day with a few more calories—this snack will add about 100 calories (418 kilojoules) to your daily intake.

What should I do if I'm having trouble coping with a Fast Day?

We have already indicated that intermittent fasting is not advisable for some people. If you experience strong headaches, excessive tiredness or feel weak or irritable on Fast Days, we advise you to stop fasting. Some people, especially those who graze a lot throughout the day, can find it difficult to limit themselves to two small meals.

We suggest you start with a month of preparation, using the menus we've developed for the Non-Fast Days, so you get used to eating only three balanced meals a day. Our meals contain slow-release carbohydrates and healthy proteins that will help you feel full. When you feel ready, you can begin the fasting program.

MEALS
ON FAST DAYS

On Fast Days, women are allowed 500 calories (2092 kilojoules). It's up to you how you allocate them throughout the day.

The 'Super 500' concept

Our personal experience only confirms the difficulty of preparing balanced meals on Fast Days. We don't have the time or inclination to spend hours in the kitchen on fasting days, especially as it encourages us to nibble—so we have developed a unique system called 'Super 500' that provides for two meals per fasting day. The advantage is that you just cook one 500-calorie (2092-kilojoule) dish, then divide the 'pot' into two portions that you eat whenever you want. We've tried to make these meals as tasty and satisfying as possible: you may not even realise that it's a Fast Day! This method minimises temptations.

The 'Super 500' recipes

In this book you'll find 30 'Super 500' recipes to choose from based on the season, but also what you have in your refrigerator.

The number of calories in these recipes has been carefully designed to provide maximum flavour and nutrients while rationing the calorie content. In the case of some recipes, we have devised extra ingredients to add to the second meal for maximum variety in the day. These seasonal meals are fresh and easy to prepare, and use the following ingredients:

- Whole grains such as quinoa and black rice: they provide a good dose of fibre, which is digested slowly and produces a feeling of fullness for longer.
- High-quality, low-fat proteins such as chicken, fish, beans and lentils, which provide essential nutrients while containing only a moderate number of calories.
- Good fats in the form of nuts, seeds or oils.
- Lots of fresh vegetables, which provide essential vitamins and minerals, but also colour, texture and flavour.

These meals allow you to optimise your intake of essential nutrients and feel full of vitality. They also allow the body and mind to get used to eating less on the Non-Fast Days.

Note: you can also make the 'Super 500' recipes in larger quantities for Non-Fast Days!

Breakfast

On Fast Days, most people prefer to skip breakfast and save their quota of calories for a light lunch and dinner. This practice has the advantage of extending the fasting period. But if you'd prefer to keep breakfast, it's perfectly acceptable.

Breakfast suggestions for Fast Days (about 100 calories/ 418 kilojoules):
- 100 g (3½ oz) berries + 100 g (3½ oz) of plain low-fat yoghurt (for those who can't manage without dairy products)
- 1 medium egg (hard-boiled or cooked without added fat) + a salad of tomato and rocket or sliced vegetables
- 200 g (7 oz) fresh fruit salad (avoid pineapple, bananas and grapes)
- 15 g (½ oz) mixed nuts (almonds, hazelnuts, walnuts, macadamia nuts, pine nuts …)

Other options are available if you plan on having a more substantial breakfast (about 200 calories/836 kilojoules) and thus prefer to skip another meal:
- 1 omelette (2 eggs) with mixed vegetables + a few salad leaves
- 30 g (1 oz) low-sugar cereal (such as All-Bran) + 100 ml (3½ fl oz) skim milk + 1 small apple cut into wedges
- 1 slice (30 g/1 oz) wholemeal bread + 1 slice (30 g/1 oz) medium-fat cheese + 40 g (1½ oz) cherry tomatoes

Tip: berries are low in sugar but high in antioxidants such as anthocyanins. When they're out of season, you can use frozen berries.

Lunch and dinner: your choice of recipes

We have also designed around 30 tasty recipes ranging from 100–300 calories (418–1255 kilojoules), so you can pick and choose for yourself! You can put together your own Fast Day menu based on what you like, what's at the market, the season and what's in your refrigerator, but also the person you'll be sharing your meal with.

THE GOLDEN RULES FOR THE NON-FAST DAYS

01

Eat balanced meals for lunch and dinner that contain unrefined carbohydrates (whole grains), proteins and vegetables.

What proportions of the different food groups should we eat? It's a subject of much debate, but as a general rule we think that you should have roughly the following proportions at each meal: 25% protein + 25% whole grains + 50% fruit and vegetables.

Eat whole grains as much as possible and limit your consumption of refined grains (white bread and rice). Give preference to fish, poultry, beans and nuts for your protein. Limit red meat to two or three times a week. Limit bacon, sausages and other cured meats as well … they contain much too much saturated fat and salt.

02

Include a small portion of protein in your breakfast (yoghurt, nuts, cheese).

Studies show that breakfasts that contain a little protein provide lasting energy for the morning and help you to avoid snacking! Good sources of protein for breakfast include dairy products, seeds, nuts and ham.

03

Eat more than five vegetables and fruits a day. Five is the minimum!

General nutritional advice suggests that we should eat at least five fruits and vegetables a day. We recommend going up to four or five serves of vegetables and two or three serves of fruit a day. Why more vegetables than fruit? Vegetables have slightly more nutrients, but above all they contain less sugar. It's important to eat the largest variety of foods possible to optimise your nutritional intake. Potatoes and chips don't count as a vegetable! We put them in the starches category. As a guide, one serve corresponds to approximately 80 g (2¾ oz).

04

Eat 'good' fats.

Fats are essential for your health. They are used to make hormones and neurotransmitters and keep our cells healthy. Diets that are very low in fat are not healthy. We believe it's better to eat real foods that are naturally low in fat.

For example, what's the difference between a no-fat yoghurt and a full-fat yoghurt? No-fat = 40 calories (167 kilojoules), while full-fat = 61 calories (255 kilojoules) and 3 g of fat. But the full-fat yoghurt tastes so much better!

Nevertheless, if you can't manage without dairy products on Fast Days, choose 'light' products so you don't load up on calories. It's okay to do this occasionally.

We prefer butter and mono-unsaturated fats such as olive oil for cooking or dressing.

Precious omega-3 fatty acids are provided by two serves of oily fish per week and a daily ration of nuts and seeds.

The menus proposed in this book are low in saturated fats because they contain limited amounts of red meat and dairy products.

The fats to avoid at all costs are trans fats and hydrogenated fats. Many studies have found a connection between these fats and an increased risk of health problems such as inflammation, cancer and even infertility. Trans fats and hydrogenated fats are solid oils produced artificially from vegetable oils. They are sometimes found in pre-cooked meals and processed foods. Read the label carefully! Oxidised fats form when oils are heated to a temperature that is too high. This damages the oil and changes its structure, transforming it into a compound that can cause inflammation in the body.

05

Stay hydrated. Water is really the best health drink.

You can drink as much water as you like. For coffee and tea lovers, there's good news—recent studies have shown that they are, in fact, good for your health, especially if you don't add sugar. They contain phytochemicals called polyphenols and other substances that potentially improve your health. That being said, high levels of caffeine can increase blood pressure and cause insomnia among the most sensitive individuals. We need to be aware of our limits!

06

Beware of sugars! Limit cakes and desserts to twice a week.

Everyone knows that fat isn't good but we often forget that sugar can be a real poison. Too much sugar increases the risk of being overweight, type 2 diabetes and dental problems. Sugar offers very little in the way of nutrients. Read labels carefully: look for the sugar content percentages. If a food contains more than 10% sugar, it is very sugary!

07

Try not to eat between meals.

By eating well-balanced meals, you can avoid snacking. The risk with snacking is eating foods that are unhealthy. And at the end of the day you forget everything you've nibbled on! The recommendation is to limit yourself to two or three meals a day (some people don't eat breakfast) plus one snack if necessary in the afternoon.

08

Limit alcohol to no more than six glasses of wine and/or beer per week. One wine = 125 ml (4 fl oz/1½ cup).

Current recommendations regarding alcohol consumption indicate a maximum of 14 units per week for women and 21 for men. It's also recommended not to drink alcohol at all on one or two days a week to let the liver recover.

We have already suggested not drinking any alcohol on Fast Days. On the Non-Fast Days, the sensible option is to limit alcohol consumption to no more than two to three units for women and three to four units for men.

What is a unit of alcohol?

A unit of alcohol corresponds to 10 ml (¼ fl oz) of pure alcohol by volume, or 8 g in weight.
For example, a unit of alcohol is roughly equivalent to:
- 230 ml (7¾ fl oz) beer
- 25 ml (¾ fl oz) spirits (40% alcohol)
- 125 ml (4 fl oz/½ cup) wine (12% alcohol)

And don't forget the most important thing: enjoy what you eat! Good food is both a pleasure and a privilege. Meals should be enjoyed and savoured! You might not always eat within the rules at every meal or on every day, but try to strike a balance over the course of the week. Your meals shouldn't become a chore or a source of guilt. Eating is a pleasure! And eating without hang-ups is a big step towards wellness.

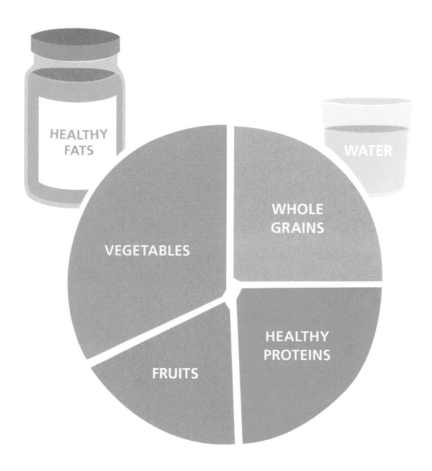

For lunch and dinner, eat balanced meals containing unrefined carbohydrates (whole grains), proteins and vegetables, with some fruit. Drink plenty of water to stay hydrated, and include small amounts of healthy fats.

ADVICE FOR THE NON-FAST DAYS

An example of a 2000-calorie (8368-kilojoule) day

Breakfast:
Wholemeal toast, fruit salad, plain yoghurt and tea/coffee.

Lunch:
Spicy chickpea salad (page 162), green salad with herbs (page 111), cheese and bread. Dessert.

Afternoon snack:
1 piece of fruit and 15 g (½ oz) nuts.

Dinner:
Energy soup (page 152). Fish tartare (page 172). A glass of wine.

Don't forget to keep an eye on the quality and quantity of the foods you eat on Non-Fast Days.

....

A note on dairy products

Milk, yoghurt and cheese are important sources of calcium. We recommend one to three servings per day. Cheese, which is high in fat, should be consumed in moderate amounts. We prefer plain yoghurt over fruit yoghurts, which contain too much sugar. It's better to sweeten your yoghurt yourself with fresh fruit or a dash of honey.

We do not recommend dairy products with 0% fat, especially on the Non-Fast Days. In dairy products, fats add flavour, enhance the feeling of fullness and contain the valuable fat-soluble vitamins A and D.

Suggestions for 'healthy' desserts

Can desserts be healthy? Yes, yes and yes! Certainly you should limit cakes and other very sugary desserts to one or two times per week, but you can enjoy fruit-based desserts on Non-Fast Days, such as: Greek-style yoghurt, fresh fruit and nuts; baked fruit gratins (apricots and plums lend themselves beautifully to these); fruit salad; and compotes and crumbles.

Among the desserts reserved for special occasions, chocolate mousse deserves a special mention (dark chocolate is an important source of magnesium and flavonols, an antioxidant phytochemical that protects cells). We are also very fond of different kinds of crumbles. Especially good are those with rolled oats and chestnut flour.

Other useful tips include using wholemeal (whole-wheat) flour to make your cakes. Also note that in many desserts, the amount of sugar can be reduced by half without changing the taste or texture.

The benefits of the Mediterranean diet combined with intermittent fasting

We recommend you follow a Mediterranean-style diet to optimise health benefits such as controlling blood sugar levels, cholesterol and blood pressure. It includes lots of fruits and vegetables, low-fat proteins, nuts, pulses, seeds and whole grains. It also includes good fats (olive oil) and omega-3 fatty acids, while limiting the saturated fats found in red meat and especially in highly processed foods (such as cakes and desserts).

Studies show that this type of diet is effective in reducing the risk of cardiovascular disease and cerebral degeneration. The combination of intermittent fasting and a Mediterranean diet can not only contribute to weight loss but also reduce the future risk of disease. Isn't that motivation enough?

.... *Did you know?* ....

Our digestive system is sometimes called the 'second brain'. It contains a whole network of neurons that communicate with the nervous system. These neurons and neurotransmitters send a message to the brain 30 minutes after eating: 'I'm not hungry anymore!' By eating more slowly, the digestive system will be able to tell the brain that you've eaten enough before it's too late!

Question: how long does it take food to reach the stomach? Answer: 5 to 6 seconds once it's been chewed and swallowed!

QUESTIONS
AND ANSWERS

Is intermittent fasting bad for your health?

The latest studies show that partial fasting produces health benefits. This way of eating is quite close to the way our ancestors ate. At times they would experience periods of abundance, while at others food would be rationed. That's why our body is made to cope with this way of eating. Most of us eat too much and too often! It is important to manage fasting in a sensible way by following the 5:2 diet. You should also make sure that you drink enough water. If in doubt, talk to your doctor about it first.

Why is the calorie intake capped at no more than 25%?

This is the threshold from which studies on animals have shown positive effects on health.

Why are men allowed to eat more than women?

Men are more muscular than women, so their metabolic rate is slightly higher. On average, a man needs 2500 calories (10,460 kilojoules) per day to maintain his weight, while a woman needs 2000 (8368 kilojoules).

Do I really have to keep within 500/600 calories a day? What if I go over a bit?

It's not the end of the world if you eat 600–700 calories (2510–2929 kilojoules) on the Fast Days, but try not to go over. Any extra calories will have an effect on your weight loss, but studies on animals still show improved health markers when the calorie restriction was only 30%.

Can I add milk or sugar to my tea/coffee?

You can add milk or sugar to your coffee, but don't forget to factor these calories into your daily total. For health reasons, we recommend that you reduce your intake of sugar as much as possible or replace sugar with a natural sweetener like stevia.

Can I shift my meal times?

Once again, the advantage of the 5:2 diet is its flexibility. As long as you don't go over 500 calories (2092 kilojoules) in 24 hours, you can eat whenever you want. Some prefer to eat one meal during the day, while others choose to keep breakfast and lunch but skip dinner. To obtain the best results, we suggest you try to have 16 hours in a row of total fasting, and therefore to make your meals at least eight hours apart (for example, 1 pm to 9 pm or 8 am to 4 pm).

Why aren't I losing weight on the diet?

The most common reason people don't lose weight on the 5:2 diet is that they overcompensate on the Non-Fast Days. We insist on the importance of eating healthy and balanced meals on the Non-Fast Days. It's not about counting calories, but remembering that high alcohol consumption combined with fatty and sugary foods is likely to put you over your daily calorie intake.

During this diet, we kept a food diary of what we ate, which was very helpful for keeping our goal in mind!

Can I adapt some of the recipes in the book?

Of course you can adapt our recipes. This is why we have detailed the number of calories/kilojoules of each ingredient and added calorie/kilojoule tables for the most commonly eaten foods.

Can I exercise on Fast Days?

You can exercise on Fast Days. In fact, recent studies show that physical activity on an empty stomach (before eating) is more efficient from the point of view of fat loss. As always, start slowly and stop immediately if you feel weak or dizzy.

Should I take vitamin or mineral supplements on Fast Days?

The vitamins and minerals we need are supposed to be supplied through our daily diet, and not by way of supplements. We've aimed to put the maximum amount of nutrients into our Fast Day recipes by using whole grains, proteins and lots of vegetables.

We have also developed menu suggestions and ideas for making the Non-Fast Days as nutritious as possible. In our opinion, if you follow our menu suggestions, you should get all the nutrients you need. Consult your doctor or nutritionist about specific concerns.

THE MAINTENANCE DIET

At the start of the diet, your weight loss goals need to be realistic and specific. You should aim for a healthy weight that you can maintain rather than an unrealistic goal.

The BMI

The aim of the maintenance diet is to have a normal body mass index (BMI), which is between 18.5 and 25 for both women and men. Body mass index[5] (BMI) is a tool used to calculate whether a person's weight is normal or not. It is calculated by dividing your weight in kilograms by your height in metres squared. Alternatively, you can multiply your weight in pounds by 4.88, then divide this by your height in feet squared.

For example: Weight = 80 kg (176.4 lb), Height = 1.83 m (6 ft)
80 / (1.83 x 1.83) = 23.9 or 176.4 x 4.88 / (6 x 6) = 23.9
A BMI below 18.4 is considered to be underweight while a score between 18.5 and 25 is ideal. When an individual's BMI is over 25, they're considered to be overweight and over 30 is considered obese.

However, the BMI is not everything. The amount of body fat is more important than BMI. Fat localised around the abdomen, called visceral fat, is a more meaningful indicator of health than the BMI. The higher the amount of visceral fat, the more vulnerable you are to cardiovascular and metabolic diseases. If your BMI is within the normal range but you have high levels of visceral fat, you may have more health problems than a person whose BMI is higher, but who has less visceral fat. Being slightly overweight (a BMI between 25 and 26.5) does not pose any additional health risks. The problem is that the more the weight goes up, the more fats tend to be stored in the form of visceral fat, which can lead to health problems.

Maintaining your weight

It is difficult to obtain precise figures, but according to some studies, 20% of people who have lost weight manage to maintain their new weight for at least one year.[6] This means that about 80% don't manage this: a totally depressing figure! Losing weight is actually only 40% of the battle; maintaining the weight loss is 60% of the work. The reason many people put weight back on is simply that they haven't adopted new permanent dietary and behavioural habits to help them maintain their weight. Many current diets effectively concentrate on weight loss. But the key to success is then knowing how to adapt the diet so you don't put the weight back on.

The 5:2 diet and weight maintenance

The 5:2 diet can easily be adapted to weight maintenance mode by shifting from two to one fasting days per week—in other words, by following a 6:1 diet instead of 5:2. There would then only be one Fast Day a week, but your diet should still be healthy and balanced on the other six days.

Some use other strategies, such as following the 5:2 diet for two weeks per month, or following the 5:2 diet after the holidays, or during specific times when you feel you've put weight back on.

Once again, the advantage of this diet is its flexibility. It's up to you to find the maintenance mode that suits you best.

How often should I weigh myself?

Some people (and there are lots of them!) weigh themselves every day. For our part, we recommend that you weigh yourself once a week, when you wake up in the morning, without any clothes on. Weight varies every day, especially for women, due to hormonal changes and fluid retention. By weighing yourself once a week, you'll have a more accurate idea of your weight loss.

After the weight loss phase, once you're in maintenance mode, it is especially important to continue to monitor your weight every week so you can respond immediately if needed …

Benefit from the positive aspects of intermittent fasting without losing weight

It's possible! Since you don't want to lose weight, you can put together meals that are a little more 'expensive' in calorie terms on the Non-Fast Days. Thus, you can allow yourself larger portions of foods high in protein, carbohydrates and nutrients such as avocado, nuts and seeds—and a little more dessert!

---

[5] The BMI is not a suitable measure for children, athletes and pregnant and lactating women.
[6] Wing, RR and Phelan, S, 'Long-term weight loss maintenance', *The American Journal of Clinical Nutrition*, 2005.

PHYSICAL
ACTIVITY

Exercise plays a vital role in keeping healthy. Contrary to common belief, exercise alone is not enough to lose weight. But the combination of exercise and the 5:2 diet is ideal for losing weight, maintaining weight and improving your health.

Intermittent fasting allows you to burn a maximum amount of fat. Combined with regular physical activity, it helps reduce body fat while building lean muscle mass.

The benefits of regular physical activity

IMPROVED INSULIN SENSITIVITY AND OTHER METABOLIC MARKERS

Insulin is an essential hormone for regulating blood sugar (glucose) levels and moving glucose into the cells of the body, where it is either stored or used to produce energy. With insulin-sensitive muscles, the body controls its blood sugar levels more effectively and is more efficient at transporting glucose to muscle cells. Exercise can help regulate cholesterol levels and levels of triglycerides (a type of fat present in the blood).

BUILDING AND MAINTAINING LEAN MUSCLE MASS
Exercise allows you to change your body composition. Body composition tells you more about overall health than weight alone. Fat stored around the stomach and internal organs (visceral fat) is bad for your health. Exercise allows this to be reduced. Muscles also burn a little more energy than fat—not enough for the difference to be significant in terms of weight loss, but probably enough to help maintain it!

PROTECTING AND STRENGTHENING BONES
Our peak bone mass is reached in early adulthood. Regular exercise allows us to maintain this bone mass and reduce the risk of osteoporosis at a later age, because physical activity helps strengthen and protect bones.

STRESS MANAGEMENT
Exercise reduces stress and releases endorphins, a natural chemical produced by the brain to reduce pain and produce a certain sense of well-being.

What sort of exercise should I do and how often?

Current recommendations advise adults to be active every day and ideally to have a combination of moderate and vigorous intensity activities throughout the week. But the essential thing is to do an exercise you like on a consistent basis and try new exercises from time to time.

VIGOROUS INTENSITY ACTIVITIES
Running, team sports (football, basketball)

MODERATE INTENSITY ACTIVITIES
Brisk walking, cycling, swimming

STRENGTH TRAINING ACTIVITIES
Yoga, Pilates, exercises with weights

If you haven't done any exercise for a long time, talk about it with your doctor before starting an exercise program. If you're starting an exercise program, you might need to shorten the length of each session at first, then gradually increase them to the recommended 30 minutes.

In the end, we need to find activities that suit us and have fun doing them! Exercise shouldn't ever be torture! Try to move more in everyday life. It can be simple things like getting off the train one stop earlier than usual, using a Pilates ball instead of a chair, or getting out of your desk chair every hour for a 5-minute walk. Taken together, these small actions make a difference. Exercise contributes to health, strength and vitality!

CALORIE
(KILOJOULE)
tables

TABLE I
GREEN VEGETABLES
calories (kilojoules) per 100 g (3½ oz)

baby salad leaves
24 (100)

English spinach
14 (59)

artichokes
34 (142)

peas
(shelled)
80 (335)

zucchini
(courgettes)
17 (71)

silverbeet
(Swiss chard)
14 (59)

fennel
31 (130)

cucumbers
12 (50)

green beans
31 (130)

broccoli
34 (142)

asparagus
24 (100)

leeks
56 (234)

cabbage
20 (84)

TABLE 11
VEGETABLES
calories (kilojoules) per 100 g (3½ oz)

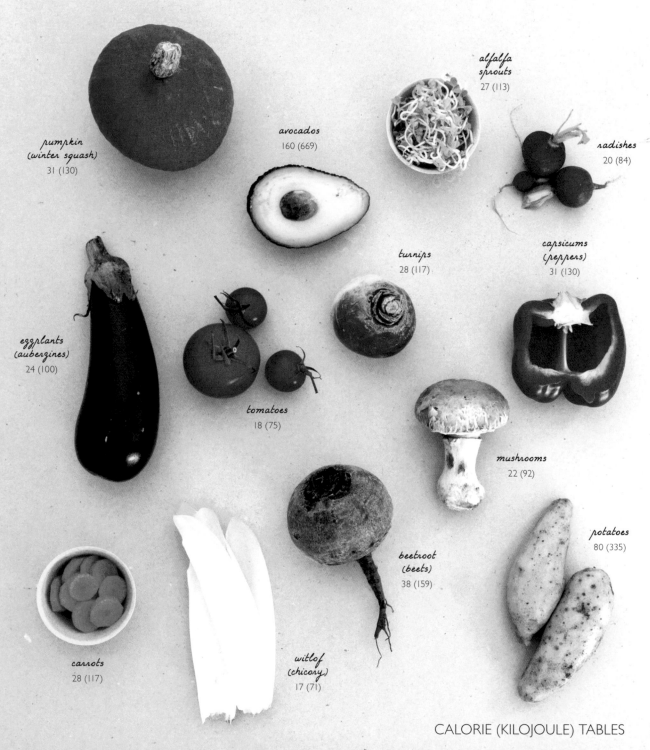

pumpkin (winter squash)
31 (130)

avocados
160 (669)

alfalfa sprouts
27 (113)

radishes
20 (84)

turnips
28 (117)

capsicums (peppers)
31 (130)

eggplants (aubergines)
24 (100)

tomatoes
18 (75)

mushrooms
22 (92)

carrots
28 (117)

witlof (chicory)
17 (71)

beetroot (beets)
38 (159)

potatoes
80 (335)

TABLE III

PULSES AND TOFU

UNCOOKED

calories (kilojoules) per 100 g (3½ oz)

chickpeas
370 (1548)

black beans
340 (1423)

tofu
120 (502)

red lentils
332 (1389)

tiny blue-green lentils
352 (1473)

kidney beans
338 (1414)

TABLE IV
STARCHES
UNCOOKED
calories (kilojoules) per 100 g (3½ oz)

bread
320 (1339)

oat bran
246 (1029)

spelt
338 (1414)

burghul
(bulgur)
344 (1439)

spelt couscous
342 (1431)

pearl barley
352 (1473)

dried rice
vermicelli
362 (1515)

kasha (roasted
buckwheat)
345 (1443)

cellophane
noodles
331 (1385)

quinoa
380 (1590)

millet
378 (1582)

rice
350 (1464)

pasta
344 (1439)

couscous
376 (1573)

TABLE V
FRUITS
calories (kilojoules) per 100 g (3½ oz)

limes (juice)
40 (167)

bananas
89 (372)

apples
52 (218)

grapes
67 (280)

raspberries
53 (222)

melons
28 (117)

plums
46 (192)

mangoes
65 (272)

strawberries
33 (138)

oranges
47 (197)

figs
74 (310)

pineapples
50 (209)

pears
57 (238)

blueberries
57 (238)

peaches
39 (163)

lemons (juice)
40 (167)

TABLE VI

DAIRY PRODUCTS

calories (kilojoules) per 100 g (3½ oz)

ricotta cheese
138 (577)

low-fat milk
50 (209)

soy cream
174 (728)

yoghurt
70 (293)

parmesan cheese
440 (1841)

*crème fraîche
(30% fat)*
293 (1226)

TABLE VII
CONDIMENTS
calories (kilojoules) per 5 g (⅛ oz) or 5 ml (1 teaspoon)

preserved
lemon (½)
9 (38)

ground
cinnamon
6 (25)

vinegar
2 (8)

chillies
5 (21)

mustard
4 (17)

kaffir lime
leaves
1 (4)

fresh ginger
3 (13)

ground
cumin
8 (33)

soy sauce
5 (21)

fennel seeds
17 (71)

capers
2 (8)

TABLE VIII

OILS, NUTS AND SEEDS

calories (kilojoules) per 5 g (⅛ oz) or 5 ml (1 teaspoon)

hazelnuts
31 (130)

flaxseed
27 (113)

butter
35 (146)

*pepitas
(pumpkin seeds)*
22 (92)

pine nuts
28 (117)

vegetable oil
45 (188)

chia seeds
30 (126)

*black or white
sesame seeds*
28 (117)

almonds
29 (121)

TABLE IX

PROTEINS
calories (kilojoules)

Meat per 100 g (3½ oz) raw	
Lamb	156 (653)
Beef tenderloin	150 (628)
Beef steak	136 (569)
Minced (ground) beef (5% fat)	137 (573)
Veal tenderloin	140 (586)
Pork tenderloin	136 (569)
Ham	107 (448)
Chicken breast	120 (502)
Chicken thigh (skinless)	145 (607)

Fish per 100 g (3½ oz) raw	
Sea bass	125 (523)
Cod	80 (335)
Hake	92 (385)
Sea bream	100 (418)
Prawns (shrimp)	80 (335)
Smoked haddock	95 (397)
Pollack	90 (377)
Mackerel	165 (690)
Mussels (with shell)	43 (180)
Red mullet	111 (464)
Scallops	87 (364)
John dory	90 (377)
Salmon	166 (695)
Smoked salmon	180 (753)
Sole	89 (372)
Bluefin tuna	108 (452)

Eggs per egg	
Egg – small	54 (226)
Egg – medium	71 (297)
Egg – large	90 (377)

See individual recipes for alternative fish suggestions.

Chapter 1

SUPER
500
RECIPES

AL DENTE VEGETABLES
& EGGS

Super **500**

SERVES 1

PREPARATION TIME: 20 MINUTES

COOKING TIME: 10 MINUTES

INGREDIENTS	CAL (KJ)
1 LARGE ZUCCHINI (COURGETTE), ABOUT 300 G (10½ OZ)	50 (209)
200 G (7 OZ) FIRM TOMATOES	36 (151)
1 FENNEL BULB, ABOUT 300 G (10½ OZ)	93 (389)
2 LARGE HARD-BOILED EGGS + 1 EGG WHITE, COOKED	199 (833)
40 G (1½ OZ/½ BUNCH) CORIANDER (CILANTRO), CHOPPED	5 (21)
½ TEASPOON GROUND CUMIN	2 (8)
2 TEASPOONS OLIVE OIL	90 (377)
25 G (1 OZ/1 LARGE HANDFUL) ROCKET (ARUGULA), WASHED & CHOPPED	6 (25)
TOTAL	481 (2013)

VARIATION FOR MEN

100 G (3½ OZ) TINNED TUNA IN WATER, DRAINED AND FLAKED	116 (485)
TOTAL	597 (2498)

GLUTEN-FREE ◆

Preparing my meal

Wash the zucchini, leave the skin on and slice into thick rounds. Steam for 10 minutes: it needs to be *al dente*. Set aside on some paper towel. Blanch the tomatoes in boiling water in a heatproof bowl for 10 seconds, then drop them into cold water. Peel the tomatoes and cut them into wedges. Set aside on paper towel. Remove the tough outer layer of the fennel bulb, wash the bulb and slice it very thinly. Shell the eggs and mash them in a bowl with a fork. Combine the mashed eggs with the coriander, cumin, 2 tablespoons of cold water and the olive oil. Season with plenty of pepper and a little salt. Arrange the vegetables on a plate, scatter the rocket over the top and dress generously with the egg sauce.

Variation for men: add the tuna before adding the sauce.

It's ready!

Speedy version: dice the fennel, zucchini and tomato, mix with the rocket and dress with sauce.

NUTRITIONAL INFO

Eggs are very nutritious and are a perfect Fast Day food. Are you worried about your cholesterol? Eggs do contain cholesterol, but recent studies show that the cholesterol in eggs does not increase cholesterol levels in the blood. Eggs can be eaten as part of a balanced diet.

QUINOA, TOMATOES,
PRESERVED LEMON & FRESH HERBS

Super
500

SERVES 1

PREPARATION TIME: 15 MINUTES

COOKING TIME: 12 MINUTES

INGREDIENTS	CAL (KJ)
1 ZUCCHINI (COURGETTE), ABOUT 250 G (9 OZ)	42 (176)
90 G (3¼ OZ) QUINOA	331 (1385)
½ (SMALL) PRESERVED LEMON	9 (38)
16 CHERRY TOMATOES, ABOUT 200 G (7 OZ)	36 (151)
1 SUCRINE (OR BABY COS) LETTUCE HEART	8 (33)
70 G (2½ OZ/1 SMALL BUNCH) HERBS (BASIL, CORIANDER/CILANTRO, TARRAGON, MINT, CHERVIL)	5 (21)
1 BULB SPRING ONION (SCALLION)	3 (13)
6–7 HAZELNUTS, ABOUT 10 G (¼ OZ)	63 (264)
TOTAL	497 (2079)

VARIATION FOR MEN

2 ZUCCHINI (COURGETTES), ABOUT 500 G (1 LB, 2 OZ)	84 (351)
105 G (3½ OZ) QUINOA	386 (1615)
TOTAL	594 (2485)

GLUTEN-FREE ◆

Preparing my meal

Wash the zucchini and cut into small pieces. Rinse the quinoa and put it in a medium saucepan with twice its volume of boiling salted water (but no oil) and the pieces of zucchini. Allow 7 minutes of cooking time before turning off the heat and letting it stand for 5 minutes. Drain. Run the preserved lemon under water to rinse off the salt, then wash the tomatoes, lettuce leaves and herbs. Chop the bulb spring onion, tomato, lettuce and lemon into small pieces (remove the seeds from the lemon). Chop the herbs. Crush the hazelnuts before toasting them for a few seconds in a dry frying pan over medium–high heat. Combine all the ingredients and season with salt and pepper. Refrigerate before eating.

It's ready!

Tip: eat it cold for the first meal and warmed slightly for the second.

Variation: if you don't have or don't like preserved lemon, you can replace it with the juice of 1 lemon (10 cal/42 kJ). Dress to your taste.

NUTRITIONAL INFO

Fresh herbs are an excellent way to add flavour without calories on your Fast Days! Basil and coriander are high in vitamin A, a fat-soluble vitamin that's essential for eye and skin health.

FRITTERS
TO GO

Super
500

SERVES 1

PREPARATION TIME: 15 MINUTES

COOKING TIME: 18 MINUTES

INGREDIENTS	CAL (KJ)
2 MEDIUM EGGS + 1 EGG WHITE	**159 (665)**
60 G (2¼ OZ/½ CUP) OAT BRAN	**147 (615)**
4 TABLESPOONS (40 G/1½ OZ) FROMAGE BLANC,	**32 (134)**
20% FAT (ALTERNATIVELY, USE QUARK	
OR YOGHURT CHEESE)	
10 CHIVES, SNIPPED	**2 (8)**
3 FLAT-LEAF (ITALIAN) PARSLEY SPRIGS, CHOPPED	**2 (8)**
2 PINCHES GROUND CUMIN	**1 (4)**
200 G (7 OZ) TOMATOES, DICED	**36 (151)**
½ YELLOW ZUCCHINI (COURGETTE),	
ABOUT 125 G (4½ OZ), DICED	**21 (88)**
¼ ONION, ABOUT 25 G (1 OZ), CHOPPED	**7 (29)**
1 TEASPOON OLIVE OIL	**45 (188)**
50 G (1¾ OZ/2 HANDFULS) MIXED SALAD LEAVES	**12 (50)**
5 G (⅛ OZ) PARMESAN CHEESE SHAVINGS	**22 (92)**
TOTAL	**486 (2032)**

VARIATION FOR MEN	
100 G (3½ OZ) HAM, FAT REMOVED	**108 (452)**
AND FINELY CHOPPED	
TOTAL	**594 (2484)**

Preparing my meal

Whisk the eggs until they're nice and frothy. Gradually add the oat bran and fromage blanc, the chives and parsley, and the cumin. Season with salt and pepper. Beat together vigorously or use an electric mixer to beat. Add the tomato, zucchini and onion. Heat a few drops of olive oil in a small frying pan. Pour one-third of the mixture into the pan and let it cook over medium heat for 3 minutes. Turn over and cook for another 3 minutes over low heat, covered. Repeat the process twice more for the rest of the mixture. Enjoy the fritters with the mixed salad leaves and sprinkled with parmesan.

Variation for men: add the ham at the same time as the tomato, zucchini and onion.

It's ready!

Tip: depending on your preferences or the size of your frying pan, you can make one, two, three or four fritters. Make them 'to order', if you prefer, and keep the rest of the mixture in the refrigerator.

Variation: replace the cumin with curry powder, Espelette pepper, chilli powder or chilli flakes for a spicier version!

This is an excellent recipe for those who can't go without brekkie or prefer to have three meals at the start.

On a personal note: I love this recipe because it is super fast, easy to make and easy to take to the office, on a picnic, or to my grandmother's house.

HOME-MADE
LASAGNE

SERVES 1

PREPARATION TIME: 25 MINUTES

COOKING TIME: 1 HOUR

INGREDIENTS	CAL (KJ)
2 LONG ZUCCHINI (COURGETTES), ABOUT 500 G (1 LB, 2 OZ)	84 (351)
1 ONION, ABOUT 100 G (3½ OZ), SLICED	28 (117)
200 G (7 OZ) EGGPLANT (AUBERGINE), DICED	48 (201)
1 TEASPOON OLIVE OIL	45 (188)
200 G (7 OZ) TOMATOES, CHOPPED	36 (151)
150 ML (5 FL OZ) TOMATO PASSATA (PURÉED TOMATOES)	24 (100)
40 G (1½ OZ) RICOTTA CHEESE	55 (230)
150 G (5½ OZ) HAM, FAT REMOVED AND CHOPPED	161 (674)
2 BASIL SPRIGS	2 (8)
50 G (1¾ OZ/2 LARGE HANDFULS) ROCKET (ARUGULA)	12 (50)
TOTAL	**495 (2070)**

VARIATION FOR MEN	
200 G (7 OZ) HAM, FAT REMOVED AND CHOPPED	204 (854)
50 G (1¾ OZ) RICOTTA CHEESE	69 (289)
100 G (3½ OZ) BISCOTTES	39 (163)
(ALTERNATIVELY, USE MELBA TOAST OR RUSKS)	
TOTAL	**591 (2473)**

Preparing my meal

Preheat the oven to 180°C (350°F). Slice the zucchini into thin slivers lengthways and cook them for 1 minute in boiling salted water in a medium saucepan. Set them aside on paper towel. In a frying pan, sauté the onion and eggplant in half the olive oil for 5 minutes over high heat. Add the tomato and tomato passata, season with salt and pepper, and simmer over medium heat for 25 minutes. Add the ricotta and ham, stir and cook for 3 minutes over low heat. In a 20 cm x 26 cm (8 in x 10½ in) baking dish (ideally), lay out a layer of zucchini slices and pour over half the sauce mixture. Arrange a second layer of zucchini on top, then the rest of the mixture and finally the last layer of zucchini. Drizzle with the remaining olive oil and bake in the oven for 25 minutes. Scatter over a few basil leaves and serve with 1 large handful of washed rocket at each meal.

Variation for men: crush the biscottes into crumbs and sprinkle over the lasagne before cooking.

It's ready!

Tips:

For dinner, you can simply reheat the dish for 5 minutes at 180°C (350°F). You can also eat this dish lukewarm. It's just as good, especially in hot weather!

Double the quantities in this recipe for a family meal that will be a treat for young and old.

On the Non-Fast Days, add 15 g (½ oz) of grated parmesan cheese to the ricotta and put 15 g (½ oz) of grated parmesan cheese on top of the lasagne with the biscottes to brown in the oven.

FRESH & EXPRESS
SALAD

Super
500

SERVES 1
PREPARATION TIME: 20 MINUTES

INGREDIENTS	CAL (KJ)
100 G (3½ OZ) BABY SALAD LEAVES	24 (100)
100 G (3½ OZ) MUSHROOMS	22 (92)
60 G (2¼ OZ) AVOCADO, DICED	96 (402)
1 TABLESPOON LEMON JUICE	3 (13)
16 CHERRY TOMATOES, ABOUT 200 G (7 OZ)	36 (151)
4 SLICES BRESAOLA, ABOUT 25 G (1 OZ)	48 (201)
(ALTERNATIVELY, USE BEEF JERKY OR OTHER DRIED MEAT)	
½ CUCUMBER, ABOUT 300 G (10½ OZ)	36 (151)
145 G (5 OZ) COOKED CHICKPEAS	161 (674)
100 G (3½ OZ) JUICY TOMATOES	18 (75)
½ PRESERVED LEMON	9 (38)
70 G (2½ OZ/1 SMALL BUNCH) HERBS (TARRAGON, CHIVES, CORIANDER/CILANTRO, BASIL), CHOPPED	6 (25)
½ TEASPOON CRUSHED, TOASTED PINE NUTS	39 (163)
TOTAL	**498 (2085)**

VARIATION FOR MEN	
6 SLICES BRESAOLA, ABOUT 35 G (1¼ OZ)	64 (268)
(ALTERNATIVELY, USE BEEF JERKY OR OTHER DRIED MEAT)	
200 G (7 OZ) COOKED CHICKPEAS	247 (1033)
TOTAL	**600 (2511)**

GLUTEN-FREE ◆

Preparing my meal

Wash and dry the salad leaves. Clean the mushrooms using damp paper towel and chop them into small pieces. Combine the mushrooms with the avocado, drizzle with lemon juice and set aside. Cut the cherry tomatoes into quarters and the bresaola into strips. Peel the cucumber, remove the seeds and dice. Rinse and drain the chickpeas. Purée the tomatoes in a food processor with the preserved lemon (remove the seeds first) and a little pepper. Combine the salad leaves with the mushrooms, avocado, cherry tomatoes, chickpeas, bresaola, cucumber and herbs.

First meal: take a portion, dress with half the tomato sauce and sprinkle with half the toasted pine nuts. Season with salt and pepper again, if necessary.

Second meal: assemble the second portion in the same way.

It's ready!

Tip: this salad is very practical and quick to make and take away … It's perfect for picnics!

Variation

Replace the chickpeas with kidney beans (see page 124 for cooking instructions).

45 G (1½ OZ) KIDNEY BEANS	153 (640)
TOTAL	**490 (2051)**
VARIATION FOR MEN	
70 G (2½ OZ) KIDNEY BEANS	238 (996)
TOTAL	**591 (2474)**

BEETROOT,
MUSHROOMS & FETA

Super
500

SERVES 1
PREPARATION TIME: 30 MINUTES
COOKING TIME: 20 MINUTES

INGREDIENTS	CAL (KJ)
40 G (1½ OZ) TINY BLUE-GREEN LENTILS	141 (590)
25 G (1 OZ) QUINOA	93 (389)
50 G (1¾ OZ/2 LARGE HANDFULS) BABY ENGLISH SPINACH, WASHED	12 (50)
200 G (7 OZ) COOKED BEETROOT (BEETS), CHOPPED	74 (310)
150 G (5½ OZ) MUSHROOMS, CLEANED AND THINLY SLICED	33 (138)
3 SLICES BRESAOLA, ABOUT 24 G (1 OZ) (ALTERNATIVELY, USE BEEF JERKY OR OTHER DRIED MEAT)	36 (151)
20 G (¾ OZ) FETA CHEESE, CRUMBLED	53 (222)
1 BASIL SPRIG, CHOPPED	1 (4)
1 SMALL FRENCH SHALLOT, CHOPPED	7 (29)
1 TEASPOON WALNUT OIL	45 (188)
TOTAL	495 (2071)

VARIATION FOR MEN	
60 G (2¼ OZ) TINY BLUE-GREEN LENTILS	212 (887)
30 G (1 OZ) QUINOA	110 (460)
TOTAL	583 (2439)

GLUTEN-FREE ◆

Preparing my meal

Cook the lentils according to the instructions on the packet and let them cool (or rinse them under cold water to stop them cooking any further and drain). Rinse the quinoa and cook it in a medium saucepan in one and a half times its volume of boiling salted water for 7 minutes. Take the pan off the heat and let it stand for 5 minutes. Pour the lentils and quinoa into a bowl. Add the baby spinach, beetroot, mushrooms, the bresaola cut into thin strips, the feta, basil and shallot. Season with salt and pepper and mix together. At serving time, add the walnut oil and mix again after correcting the seasoning if necessary.

It's ready!

My advice: so the mushrooms retain their freshness, I suggest you slice them very thinly over the plate using a mandoline at the last moment for each meal. They'll stay nice and crisp and be a lovely colour!

Variation: if you don't like cooked beetroot, you can replace it with thinly sliced raw beetroot or 180 g (6¼ oz) grated carrots—the calories will be the same.

Speedy tip: if you already have cooked lentils and quinoa in the refrigerator, this recipe will be super quick to assemble.

On a personal note: thanks to Chloé for this super, balanced recipe with a touch of indulgence with the feta!

PASTA
& VEGETABLES

SERVES 1
PREPARATION TIME: 30 MINUTES
COOKING TIME: 36 MINUTES

INGREDIENTS	CAL (KJ)
100 G (3½ OZ) FENNEL	31 (130)
½ ZUCCHINI (COURGETTE), ABOUT 125 G (4½ OZ)	21 (88)
½ EGGPLANT (AUBERGINE), ABOUT 100 G (3½ OZ)	24 (100)
100 G (3½ OZ) MUSHROOMS	22 (92)
100 G (3½ OZ) BABY ENGLISH SPINACH	24 (100)
200 G (7 OZ) TOMATOES	36 (151)
1 TEASPOON OLIVE OIL	45 (188)
2 PINCHES CAYENNE PEPPER	1 (4)
2 PINCHES GROUND CUMIN	1 (4)
85 G (3 OZ/1 CUP) PASTA OF YOUR CHOICE	293 (1226)
TOTAL	**498 (2083)**

VARIATION FOR MEN	
110 G (3¾ OZ/1¼ CUP) PASTA	380 (1590)
TOTAL	**585 (2447)**

Preparing my meal

Prepare the vegetables. Remove the fennel's tough outer layer. Wash the zucchini, fennel, eggplant and mushrooms, and chop them into small pieces. Steam the zucchini, fennel and eggplant for 15 minutes. Wash the baby spinach and process 25 g (1 oz) of it in a food processor with the tomatoes, olive oil, some salt and pepper and 2 tablespoons of water. Pour this sauce into a frying pan and simmer for 10 minutes over medium heat. Add the cayenne pepper, cumin, mushrooms and steamed vegetables, and cook over low heat for 10 minutes. Meanwhile, cook the portion of pasta (half per meal) for 1–2 minutes less than the time indicated on the packet. Take 1 small ladleful of pasta water and add it to the vegetable sauce. Set aside half of the sauce for the second meal. Drain the pasta and add it to the frying pan. Stir and continue to cook for 1 minute. Serve immediately with the remaining fresh baby spinach mixed in at the last moment. Do the same for the second meal.

It's ready!

Tip: if you prefer you can cook all the pasta at once and reheat it very gently for the second meal—but I'm always afraid of overcooking the pasta, so I prefer to do it in two batches!

NUTRITIONAL INFO
You can use quinoa or buckwheat pasta for a gluten-free recipe.

MINESTRONE

Super
500

SERVES 1

PREPARATION TIME: 25 MINUTES

COOKING TIME: 40 MINUTES

INGREDIENTS	CAL (KJ)
35 G (1¼ OZ) PEARL BARLEY	123 (515)
35 G (1¼ OZ) QUINOA	128 (536)
1 SMALL ROSEMARY SPRIG	1 (4)
1 GARLIC CLOVE, CHOPPED	4 (17)
60 G (2¼ OZ/3 LARGE HANDFULS) BASIL, CHOPPED	3 (13)
½ CARROT, ABOUT 50 G (1¾ OZ)	22 (92)
½ FIRM ZUCCHINI (COURGETTE), ABOUT 125 G (4½ OZ)	21 (88)
1 LEEK, PALE PART ONLY, ABOUT 75 G (2½ OZ)	42 (176)
½ ONION, ABOUT 50 G (1¾ OZ)	14 (59)
1 PINCH CHILLI POWDER	1 (4)
½ REDUCED-FAT CHICKEN STOCK CUBE	6 (25)
1 TEASPOON TOMATO PASTE (CONCENTRATED PURÉE)	9 (38)
50 G (1¾ OZ/⅓ CUP) SHELLED PEAS, OR 125 G (4½ OZ) IN THEIR PODS	40 (167)
50 G (1¾ OZ) SHELLED BROAD BEANS	44 (184)
5 G (⅛ OZ) FRESHLY GRATED PARMESAN CHEESE	22 (92)
½ TEASPOON BLACK SESAME SEEDS	13 (54)
TOTAL	**493 (2064)**

VARIATION FOR MEN	
60 G (2¼ OZ) QUINOA	219 (916)
TOTAL	**584 (2444)**

Preparing my meal

Rinse the barley and quinoa under cold water and put them in a heavy-based saucepan with 750 ml (26 fl oz/3 cups) of cold water. Add the rosemary, garlic and half the basil. Cook over low heat, covered, for 15 minutes. Prepare the vegetables: cut the carrot into pieces, cut the zucchini into cubes, slice the leek into short lengths, and cut the onion into segments. Remove the lid from the saucepan and add the chilli, the half stock cube, the tomato paste, carrot, peas, leek and onion. Season with salt and pepper. Replace the lid and cook for a further 15 minutes over low heat. Uncover again, add the zucchini and broad beans, and cook for a further 10 minutes. Serve immediately with half the remaining basil, and sprinkled with freshly grated parmesan and black sesame seeds (put aside a little of the parmesan, sesame seeds and basil for the second serving). Note that the minestrone should be served runny, not gluey. If necessary, add a little water during cooking so there's always some in the pot.

It's ready!

My advice: to make sure the second serving isn't overcooked, strain the minestrone once it's cooked and keep the broth separate. Reheat very gently, reincorporating the hot broth. This recipe is ideal to cook for the whole family.

Tip: I grate my parmesan using a 'magic' Microplane® grater that creates flakes of parmesan so thin and light that the volume expands without inflating the calories!

NUTRITIONAL INFO

Barley is a good source of beta-glucans, a soluble fibre that helps keep cholesterol levels under control.

WINTER SOUP

Super
500

SERVES 1
PREPARATION TIME: 25 MINUTES
COOKING TIME: 35 MINUTES

INGREDIENTS	CAL (KJ)
80 G (2¾ OZ) POTATOES	64 (268)
100 G (3½ OZ) PUMPKIN (WINTER SQUASH)	31 (130)
80 G (2¾ OZ) JERUSALEM ARTICHOKES	58 (243)
1 SMALL TURNIP, ABOUT 100 G (3½ OZ)	28 (117)
1 LEEK, PALE PART ONLY, ABOUT 75 G (2½ OZ)	42 (176)
100 G (3½ OZ) SAVOY CABBAGE	26 (109)
75 G (2½ OZ/½ BUNCH) FLAT-LEAF (ITALIAN) PARSLEY, CHOPPED	5 (21)
50 G (1¾ OZ) PORK TENDERLOIN, CHOPPED	68 (285)
5 G (⅛ OZ) FRESHLY GRATED PARMESAN CHEESE	22 (92)
1 TEASPOON HAZELNUT OIL	45 (188)
30 G (1 OZ) KASHA (ROASTED BUCKWHEAT)	105 (439)
TOTAL	**494 (2068)**

VARIATION FOR MEN	
75 G (2½ OZ) PORK TENDERLOIN	101 (423)
50 G (1¾ OZ) KASHA (ROASTED BUCKWHEAT)	176 (736)
TOTAL	**598 (2503)**

GLUTEN-FREE ◆

Preparing my meal

Prepare the vegetables: chop the potatoes, pumpkin, Jerusalem artichokes and turnip into small cubes, cut the leek into short lengths and the cabbage into strips. Heat 1.25 litres (44 fl oz/5 cups) of salted water in a saucepan over medium heat and add the vegetables, parsley and pork pieces. Season lightly with pepper. Cook on a low simmer for 30 minutes.

First meal: serve the soup steaming hot with a little parmesan and the hazelnut oil.

Second meal: reheat the soup and add the kasha to the boiling soup. It will stay a little crunchy, but it's delicious that way.

It's ready!

Veggie version: leave out the pork and increase the kasha in the dish.

45 G (1½ OZ) KASHA (ROASTED BUCKWHEAT)	156 (653)
TOTAL	**477 (1996)**

VARIATION FOR MEN	
75 G (2½ OZ) KASHA (ROASTED BUCKWHEAT)	264 (1105)
TOTAL	**585 (2448)**

Divide the kasha between the two meals.

Shopping: you'll find kasha (roasted buckwheat) in your local organic supermarket or online.

My advice: you can certainly prepare the soup using all the ingredients for the whole day. But be careful to add only half the kasha for each meal—otherwise, it will be way overcooked for the second meal.

NUTRITIONAL INFO

Kasha is a gluten-free whole grain with a low glycaemic index (GI) ranking. It's great for making you feel fuller for longer.

BLACK BEAN
SOUP

Super
500

SERVES 1
PREPARATION TIME: 25 MINUTES
COOKING TIME: 2 HOURS
SOAKING TIME: OVERNIGHT

INGREDIENTS	CAL (KJ)
80 G (2¾ OZ) DRIED BLACK TURTLE BEANS	278 (1163)
750 ML (26 FL OZ/3 CUPS) HOT CHICKEN STOCK, FAT REMOVED	12 (50)
½ ONION, ABOUT 50 G (1¾ OZ), CHOPPED	14 (59)
½ TEASPOON GROUND CUMIN	2 (8)
½ RED CHILLI, SEEDED AND FINELY CHOPPED	1 (4)
½ GARLIC CLOVE, CHOPPED	2 (8)
8 CORIANDER (CILANTRO) SPRIGS, CHOPPED	3 (13)
JUICE AND GRATED ZEST OF ½ UNTREATED (ORGANIC) LIME	5 (21)
100 G (3½ OZ) TOMATOES, WASHED AND DICED	18 (75)
½ RED CAPSICUM (PEPPER), ABOUT 100 G (3½ OZ), WASHED AND DICED	31 (130)
50 G (1¾ OZ/2 HANDFULS) BABY ENGLISH SPINACH, COARSELY CHOPPED	12 (50)
25 G (1 OZ/1 SLICE) HAM, FAT REMOVED AND CHOPPED	30 (126)
½ MEDIUM HARD-BOILED EGG, CHOPPED	35 (146)
1 TEASPOON OLIVE OIL	45 (188)
TOTAL	**488 (2041)**

VARIATION FOR MEN	
100 G (3½ OZ) DRIED BLACK TURTLE BEANS	347 (1452)
50 G (2 OZ/2 SLICES) HAM, FAT REMOVED AND CHOPPED	60 (251)
TOTAL	**587 (2455)**

Preparing my meal

Soak the beans in water overnight in the refrigerator. Rinse and drain them. Add the beans to a medium saucepan with the hot stock, onion, cumin, chilli and garlic, half the coriander, and salt and pepper. Bring to the boil and simmer very gently for 2 hours. Taste the beans: they should melt in your mouth. Add the lime juice and some salt, and purée the soup. Thin it out with a little boiling water, if necessary. Serve each portion in a deep plate or bowl. For the first serving, add half the tomato, capsicum, baby spinach, remaining coriander and the lime zest. Set the other half of these ingredients aside for the second serving. Sprinkle over a few drops of olive oil when serving.

First meal: serve with the ham.

Second meal: serve topped with the egg.

It's ready!

Speedy tip: you can make this soup with tinned kidney beans instead of the turtle beans. Method: simmer 250 ml (9 fl oz/1 cup) stock for 10 minutes with all the other ingredients (garlic, onion, cumin, chilli, half the coriander, salt and pepper) and then purée with the kidney beans.

200 G (7 OZ) KIDNEY BEANS	280 (1172)
TOTAL	**490 (2050)**
VARIATION FOR MEN	
245 G (9 OZ) KIDNEY BEANS	344 (1439)
TOTAL	**584 (2442)**

NUTRITIONAL INFO
Pulses are an excellent source of soluble fibre, which helps maintain a healthy digestive system.

MY RATATOUILLE
FOR THE DAY

Super
500

SERVES 1

PREPARATION TIME: 20 MINUTES

COOKING TIME: 4 HOURS, 5 MINUTES

INGREDIENTS	CAL (KJ)
30 G (1 OZ/2 LARGE HANDFULS) CORIANDER (CILANTRO) LEAVES	4 (17)
1 ONION, ABOUT 100 G (3½ OZ)	28 (117)
2 ZUCCHINI (COURGETTES), ABOUT 500 G (1 LB, 2 OZ)	84 (351)
1 LARGE EGGPLANT (AUBERGINE), ABOUT 300 G (10 ½ OZ)	72 (301)
1 TEASPOON OLIVE OIL	45 (188)
240 G (8¾ OZ) TINNED PEELED TOMATOES	50 (209)
1 PINCH GROUND CUMIN	1 (4)
1 PINCH PAPRIKA	1 (4)
1 LARGE RED CAPSICUM (PEPPER), ABOUT 200 G (7 OZ)	62 (259)
1 LARGE YELLOW CAPSICUM (PEPPER), ABOUT 200 G (7 OZ)	62 (259)
1 LARGE EGG	90 (377)
TOTAL	**499 (2086)**

VARIATION FOR MEN	
2 LARGE EGGS	180 (753)
TOTAL	**589 (2462)**

GLUTEN-FREE ◆

Preparing my meal

Wash and prepare the vegetables and herbs: coarsely chop the coriander, cut the onion into wedges, and cut the zucchini and eggplant into large cubes. In a flameproof casserole dish, heat the olive oil and sauté the onion over high heat for 5 minutes. Once the onion is lightly browned, add the tomatoes with their juice, the zucchini and eggplant. Season with salt and pepper, and add the cumin, coriander and paprika. Cook over very low heat, covered, for 2 hours. Meanwhile, heat the griller and grill the capsicums until they are quite black on all sides. Place them in an airtight bag or a plastic container and let them cool, then remove the skin and the seeds. Slice them into strips. After the first 2 hours of cooking the ratatouille, add the capsicums and cook uncovered for another 2 hours over very low heat. Watch carefully to make sure it does not burn (take it off the heat if it does).

Second meal: reheat the ratatouille gently, cook one soft-boiled egg (approximately 5–6 minutes, then peel under cold running water), and serve the ratatouille in a bowl with the egg on top.

Variation for men: serve with one soft-boiled egg at each meal.

It's ready!

Tip: make the ratatouille the day before and reheat very gently.

NUTRITIONAL INFO

Cooked tomatoes are a rich source of lycopene, a powerful antioxidant that has been linked with a reduced risk of heart disease and some cancers. Cooked and tinned tomatoes actually contain more lycopene than fresh tomatoes!

On a personal note: I often make this dish for the whole family, doubling the quantities. My portion size is still ideal, as it's one-quarter of the total weight. Everyone eats the same thing, which makes it much easier.

QUINOA
& WINTER VEGETABLES

Super
500

SERVES 1

PREPARATION TIME: 20 MINUTES

COOKING TIME: 19 MINUTES

INGREDIENTS	CAL (KJ)
80 G (2¾ OZ) QUINOA	**294 (1230)**
250 G (9 OZ) ZUCCHINI (COURGETTES)	**42 (176)**
150 G (5½ OZ) BUTTERNUT PUMPKIN (SQUASH), SKIN REMOVED	**75 (314)**
150 G (5½ OZ) CHINESE CABBAGE (WONG BOK)	**18 (75)**
1–2 PINCHES GROUND CUMIN	**1 (4)**
10 G (¼ OZ) PEPITAS (PUMPKIN SEEDS), CHOPPED	**60 (251)**
GRATED ZEST OF 1 UNTREATED (ORGANIC) LIME	**2 (8)**
25 G (1 OZ/1 LARGE HANDFUL) ROCKET (ARUGULA)	**6 (25)**
TOTAL	**498 (2083)**

VARIATION FOR MEN	
105 G (3½ OZ) QUINOA	**386 (1615)**
50 G (1¾ OZ/2 LARGE HANDFULS) ROCKET (ARUGULA)	**12 (50)**
TOTAL	**596 (2493)**

GLUTEN-FREE ◆

Preparing my meal

Rinse the quinoa and cook it in one and a half times its volume of boiling salted water (but no oil). Pour in the quinoa when the water is boiling and allow 7 minutes to cook it *al dente* so it can be reheated a little later without overcooking. Turn off the heat and let it stand for 5 minutes. Run the quinoa under cold water to stop it cooking any further and drain. Meanwhile, wash all the vegetables, chop the zucchini and pumpkin into small cubes, and the cabbage into strips. Heat a large frying pan without adding any oil and cook the vegetables over high heat for 5 minutes, stirring frequently. Reduce the heat, add 3 tablespoons of water and the cumin and cook for another 2 minutes, stirring. Season with salt and pepper. Combine the vegetables with the quinoa and add the chopped pepitas. At meal time, gently reheat one portion, adding 1–2 tablespoons of water if necessary. Before eating, sprinkle with lime zest, and serve with the rocket.

It's ready!

Variation: replace the butternut pumpkin and Chinese cabbage with the following alternatives:

	CAL (KJ)
150 G (5½ OZ) PUMPKIN (WINTER SQUASH)	**47 (197)**
150 G (5½ OZ) SAVOY CABBAGE	**39 (163)**
TOTAL	**491 (2054)**
VARIATION FOR MEN	**589 (2464)**

NUTRITIONAL INFO

Quinoa is not a grain but a seed! It's a super food that's high in protein (14%), and a source of fibre, magnesium and iron.

SPELT
RISOTTO

Super
500

SERVES 1

PREPARATION TIME: 15 MINUTES

COOKING TIME: 35 MINUTES

INGREDIENTS	CAL (KJ)
1 BULB SPRING ONION (SCALLION)	3 (13)
1 TEASPOON OLIVE OIL	45 (188)
85 G (3 OZ) SPELT	287 (1201)
500 ML (17 FL OZ/2 CUPS) HOT CHICKEN STOCK, FAT REMOVED	8 (33)
90 G (3¼ OZ) SHELLED PEAS, OR 225 G (8 OZ) IN THEIR PODS	72 (301)
120 G (4¼ OZ) MUSHROOMS	26 (109)
2 SLICES BRESAOLA, ABOUT 16 G (½ OZ), CHOPPED (ALTERNATIVELY, USE BEEF JERKY OR OTHER DRIED MEAT)	24 (100)
25 G (1 OZ/1 LARGE HANDFUL) ROCKET (ARUGULA)	6 (25)
5 G (⅛ OZ) FRESHLY GRATED PARMESAN CHEESE	22 (92)
2 BASIL SPRIGS	2 (8)
TOTAL	**495 (2070)**

VARIATION FOR MEN	
115 G (4 OZ) SPELT	388 (1623)
700 ML (24 FL OZ) CHICKEN STOCK, FAT REMOVED	11 (46)
TOTAL	**599 (2505)**

Preparing my meal

Chop the stem and bulb of the onion into small pieces. Heat the olive oil in a large frying pan over medium heat, add the onion, and sauté for 2 minutes. Add the spelt and stir so the grains are well coated. Season with salt and a little pepper and add the hot stock. Simmer, covered, over low heat for 15 minutes. Add the peas, cover and cook for a further 10 minutes. Clean the mushrooms and chop them into pieces. Add them to the pan and cook for a further 5 minutes. Stir occasionally to obtain a creamy consistency. Serve each portion with the bresaola, rocket, a little parmesan and basil leaves. Season with salt and pepper, if necessary.

It's ready!

My advice: after serving the first portion, I suggest spreading out the rest of the risotto on a cold plate to stop it cooking any further. Reheat it very gently in a saucepan with 100 ml (3½ fl oz) of boiling water for a few minutes for the second portion.

Veggie version: double the quantity of parmesan cheese and leave out the bresaola.

TOTAL	493 (2063)
VARIATION FOR MEN	597 (2498)

Shopping: spelt can be easily found in supermarkets and organic food stores.

SUMMER
SOUP

Super
500

SERVES 1
PREPARATION TIME: 25 MINUTES
COOKING TIME: 40 MINUTES

INGREDIENTS	CAL (KJ)
80 G (2¾ OZ) SCALLOPS, CORAL (ROE) REMOVED	70 (293)
1 TEASPOON CANOLA OIL	45 (188)
GRATED ZEST OF 1 UNTREATED (ORGANIC) LIME	2 (8)
100 G (3½ OZ) ASPARAGUS, CHOPPED	22 (92)
1 ZUCCHINI (COURGETTE), ABOUT 250 G (9 OZ), DICED	42 (176)
2 CARROTS, ABOUT 200 G (7 OZ), DICED	82 (343)
½ FENNEL BULB, ABOUT 150 G (5½ OZ), DICED	47 (197)
50 G (1¾ OZ) POTATO, DICED	40 (167)
50 G (1¾ OZ/⅓ CUP) SHELLED PEAS,	40 (167)
OR 125 G (4½ OZ) IN THEIR PODS	
150 G (5½ OZ/1 BUNCH) FLAT-LEAF (ITALIAN) PARSLEY	10 (42)
25 G (1 OZ) BABY ENGLISH SPINACH	6 (25)
1 BAY LEAF	1 (4)
25 G (1 OZ) QUINOA	92 (385)
TOTAL	**499 (2087)**

VARIATION FOR MEN	
50 G (1¾ OZ/¼ CUP) QUINOA	184 (770)
TOTAL	**591 (2472)**

GLUTEN-FREE ◆

Preparing my meal

Always buy very fresh scallops for eating raw. Chop the cleaned scallops into small pieces and marinate them in the refrigerator in the canola oil with half the lime zest, salt and pepper. Make the soup: heat 750 ml (26 fl oz/3 cups) of salted water in a medium saucepan. Add all of the vegetables (asparagus, zucchini, carrots, fennel and potato), the shelled peas, parsley, baby spinach and bay leaf. Lightly season with pepper. Cook on a low simmer for 30 minutes.

First meal: place the scallops in the bottom of a deep plate or bowl and pour over a portion of hot broth and vegetables.

Second meal: rinse the quinoa and cook it in one and a half times its volume of boiling salted water (without oil) for 7 minutes. Take off the heat and let it stand for 5 minutes uncovered. Add the quinoa to the reheated soup, sprinkle with the rest of the lime zest and serve immediately.

It's ready!

Veggie version: leave out the scallops and increase the quantity of quinoa.

40 G (1½ OZ) QUINOA	147 (615)
TOTAL	**484 (2025)**

VARIATION FOR MEN	
70 G (2½ OZ) QUINOA	258 (1079)
TOTAL	**595 (2489)**

Divide the quinoa between the two meals.

NUTRITIONAL INFO
Scallops are a rich source of the amino acid tryptophan, which can help to manage mood swings and assist with improving sleep.

BLACK RICE,
PEAS, ASPARAGUS & MINT

SERVES 1

PREPARATION TIME: 20 MINUTES

COOKING TIME: 1 HOUR

INGREDIENTS	CAL (KJ)
55 G (2 OZ) BLACK RICE	193 (808)
150 G (5½ OZ) WHITE ASPARAGUS	36 (151)
80 G (2¾ OZ/½ CUP) SHELLED PEAS, OR 200 G (7 OZ) IN THEIR PODS	64 (268)
25 G (1 OZ/1 LARGE HANDFUL) ROCKET (ARUGULA)	6 (25)
8 FRESH MINT LEAVES, CHOPPED	1 (4)
12 CHERRY TOMATOES, ABOUT 150 G (5½ OZ/1 CUP), CHOPPED	24 (100)
1 TEASPOON OLIVE OIL	45 (188)
40 G (1½ OZ) TINNED TUNA IN WATER, DRAINED AND FLAKED	48 (201)
1 MEDIUM EGG	71 (297)
TOTAL	**488 (2042)**

VARIATION FOR MEN	
85 G (3 OZ) BLACK RICE	298 (1247)
TOTAL	**593 (2481)**

GLUTEN-FREE ◆

Preparing my meal

Pour the rice into a small saucepan with two and a half times its volume of cold water. Add salt and cook for 45 minutes to 1 hour over low heat (see page 124). Meanwhile, peel the asparagus and cut off the woody ends. Wash the peas and steam them with the asparagus for 10 minutes. Once the rice is cooked, rinse it under cold water and drain. Let the vegetables cool, then cut the asparagus into short lengths and add it to the rice with the peas. Add the rocket and mint, the tomato, olive oil, salt and pepper, and mix well. Refrigerate before eating.

First meal: take a portion and add the tuna.

Second meal: cook a soft-boiled egg (5–6 minutes), peel it under cold running water and place on top of the dish.

It's ready!

My advice: if the salad is a little dry with the tuna, add 1–2 tablespoons of warm water and mix thoroughly or purée half the tomatoes to make a little sauce.

Shopping: you'll find black rice in organic food stores.

NUTRITIONAL INFO
Black rice is a rich source of anthocyanins, an antioxidant that helps protect against the risk of cardiovascular disease, among other things.

Variation: replace the tuna with the following alternative:

45 G (1½ OZ) TOFU	54 (226)
TOTAL	**494 (2067)**
VARIATION FOR MEN	**599 (2506)**

SCALLOPS
WITH PESTO

Super
500

SERVES 1
PREPARATION TIME: 15 MINUTES
COOKING TIME: 20 MINUTES

INGREDIENTS	CAL (KJ)
5–6 SCALLOPS (ABOUT 180 G/6¼ OZ), CORAL (ROE) REMOVED	157 (657)
JUICE AND GRATED ZEST OF 1 UNTREATED (ORGANIC) LIME	10 (42)
50 G (1¾ OZ) ZUCCHINI (COURGETTE), CHOPPED	9 (38)
25 G (1 OZ/1 LARGE HANDFUL) ROCKET (ARUGULA)	6 (25)
1 MINT SPRIG	1 (4)
1 TEASPOON OLIVE OIL	45 (188)
300 G (10½ OZ) EDAMAME BEANS, ABOUT 140 G (5 OZ) SHELLED	178 (745)
1 KALE LEAF, ABOUT 10 G (¼ OZ)	5 (21)
75 G (2½ OZ) COOKED CHICKPEAS	84 (351)
TOTAL	**495 (2071)**

VARIATION FOR MEN	
6–7 SCALLOPS (ABOUT 210 G/7½ OZ), CORAL (ROE) REMOVED	183 (766)
340 G (12 OZ) EDAMAME BEANS, ABOUT 160 G (5½ OZ) SHELLED	203 (849)
115 G (4 OZ) COOKED CHICKPEAS	128 (536)
TOTAL	**590 (2469)**

GLUTEN-FREE ◆

Preparing my meal

Put the cleaned scallops on a small plate, sprinkle over half the lime juice and season with salt and pepper. Cover them and place in the refrigerator while making the rest of the dish. Steam the zucchini for 10 minutes. To make the pesto, purée the zucchini in a food processor with half the rocket, the remaining lime juice, half the mint, the olive oil, 250 ml (9 fl oz/1 cup) of water and salt and pepper. Meanwhile, bring a saucepan of salted water to the boil and drop in the edamame beans for 2–3 minutes if they are frozen; 45 seconds if they have already thawed; and 8–9 minutes if they are fresh. They need to stay quite crisp. Drain and shell the beans, make up the weight indicated for the recipe and give the rest to your children, friends, neighbours or pets with a dash of sweet soy sauce … Delicious. Remove the thick stem of the kale and cut the leaf into pieces. Rinse and drain the chickpeas and combine them with the beans, kale and remaining rocket leaves. Chop the rest of the mint leaves, and add them to the salad with the lime zest, salt and pepper.

First meal: serve half the scallops raw, especially if they are very fresh, with the salad and pesto.

Second meal: sear the scallops in a frying pan over medium–high heat for 1 minute on each side and serve immediately with the rest of the salad and pesto.

It's ready!

Variation: you can eat all of the scallops cooked or all raw! It's up to you. Both ways are really very good.

Shopping: edamame beans are a variety of soybean that are increasingly found on supermarket shelves or in the freezer section. Kale is a kind of curly-leafed cabbage, packed with vitamins but a little bitter! It's something you'll see more and more in stores and supermarkets.

THAI SALAD

Super **500**

SERVES 1

PREPARATION TIME: 15 MINUTES

COOKING TIME: 5 MINUTES

INGREDIENTS	CAL (KJ)
60 G (2¼ OZ) CELLOPHANE NOODLES	199 (833)
1 CM (½ IN) PIECE OF GINGER, GRATED	2 (8)
½ RED CHILLI, SEEDED AND FINELY CHOPPED	1 (4)
1 TABLESPOON SOY SAUCE	10 (42)
½ SMALL FRENCH SHALLOT, CHOPPED	3 (13)
GRATED ZEST AND JUICE OF 1 UNTREATED (ORGANIC) LIME	10 (42)
1 TEASPOON GRAPESEED OIL	45 (188)
50 ML (1½ FL OZ) COCONUT WATER	10 (42)
50 G (1¾ OZ) MANGO, DICED	32 (134)
2 BULB SPRING ONIONS (SCALLIONS), ABOUT 10 G (¼ OZ), BULBS AND STEMS THINLY SLICED	5 (21)
40 G (1½ OZ) BEAN SPROUTS, RINSED AND DRAINED	12 (50)
8 CORIANDER (CILANTRO) SPRIGS AND 2 MINT SPRIGS, CHOPPED	3 (13)
100 G (3½ OZ) COOKED PRAWNS (SHRIMP), PEELED AND CHOPPED	80 (335)
75 G (2½ OZ) RAW BLUEFIN TUNA, VERY FRESH, DICED	81 (339)
25 G (1 OZ/1 HANDFUL) BABY SALAD LEAVES	6 (25)
TOTAL	**499 (2089)**

VARIATION FOR MEN

80 G (2¾ OZ) CELLOPHANE NOODLES	265 (1109)
100 G (3½ OZ) RAW BLUEFIN TUNA, VERY FRESH, DICED	108 (452)
TOTAL	**592 (2478)**

Preparing my meal

Put the cellophane noodles in a large bowl and pour over boiling water. Let them stand for 5 minutes, then drain. Return the noodles to the bowl, cutting them up roughly with scissors. Make the dressing by combining the ginger, chilli, soy sauce, shallot, lime zest and juice, grapeseed oil and coconut water. Taste and add salt and pepper, if necessary. Pour the dressing over the noodles and mix well. Add the mango, onions, bean sprouts and herbs and mix together.

First meal: add the prawn chunks to one portion.

Second meal: mix the raw tuna with the rest of the noodles. Serve each meal with a few salad leaves.

It's ready!

Tip: this dish is even better after it has marinated for a few hours in the refrigerator. It's even better to make it the day before and mix in the herbs and salad leaves just before eating.

NUTRITIONAL INFO

Prawns are low in fat and a rich source of protein—100 g (3½ oz) prawns contains about 20 g (¾ oz) protein and less than 2 g (¹⁄₁₆ oz) fat.

BURGHUL
& RAW SALMON

Super
500

SERVES 1

PREPARATION TIME: 15 MINUTES

COOKING TIME: 12 MINUTES

INGREDIENTS	CAL (KJ)
70 G (2½ OZ) BURGHUL (BULGUR)	240 (1004)
½ TEASPOON CIDER VINEGAR	5 (21)
1 TEASPOON OLIVE OIL	45 (188)
½ CUCUMBER, ABOUT 300 G (10½ OZ), PEELED AND DICED	36 (151)
10 G (¼ OZ) CHIVES, SNIPPED	3 (13)
90 G (3¼ OZ) RAW SALMON, VERY FRESH	150 (628)
75 G (2½ OZ/1 SMALL BUNCH) SORREL, WASHED AND COARSELY CHOPPED	19 (79)
TOTAL	**498 (2084)**

VARIATION FOR MEN	
90 G (3¼ OZ/½ CUP) BURGHUL (BULGUR)	309 (1293)
110 G (3¾ OZ) RAW SALMON, VERY FRESH	183 (766)
TOTAL	**600 (2511)**

Preparing my meal

Cook the burghul in two and a half times its volume of boiling salted water, uncovered, over medium heat for 7 minutes. Let it stand off the heat for 5 minutes. Drain and set aside. Dress the burghul with the vinegar and olive oil, and season with salt and pepper. Add the cucumber and chives. Set aside in the refrigerator. Clean and cut the salmon into small cubes, season them with salt and pepper, and set aside in the refrigerator. At the last minute, combine the burghul with the sorrel. Serve with the cubes of salmon on top.

It's ready!

Note: salmon has many more calories than white fish.

Variation: replace the salmon with raw cod and add more burghul (bulgur).

150 G (5½ OZ) COD, VERY FRESH	120 (502)
75 G (2¾ OZ) BURGHUL	257 (1075)
TOTAL	**485 (2029)**

VARIATION FOR MEN

150 G (5½ OZ) COD, VERY FRESH	120 (502)
105 G (3½ OZ) BURGHUL	360 (1506)
TOTAL	**588 (2460)**

Variation 2: replace the sorrel with baby English spinach.

On a personal note: thank you Charlotte for your photos but also for this fantastic recipe!

LENTIL
& FISH
SALAD

Super
500

SERVES 1

PREPARATION TIME: 15 MINUTES

COOKING TIME: 20 MINUTES

INGREDIENTS	CAL (KJ)
110 G (3¾ OZ/½ CUP) LENTILS	**387 (1619)**
1 BULB SPRING ONION (SCALLION), STEM AND BULB THINLY SLICED	**3 (13)**
40 G (1½ OZ/½ BUNCH) CORIANDER (CILANTRO), CHOPPED	**5 (21)**
JUICE AND GRATED ZEST OF 1 UNTREATED (ORGANIC) LEMON	**12 (50)**
1 TABLESPOON MUSTARD	**10 (42)**
1 TEASPOON OLIVE OIL	**45 (188)**
40 G (1½ OZ) RAW SMOKED HADDOCK	**38 (159)**
TOTAL	**500 (2092)**

VARIATION FOR MEN	
100 G (3½ OZ) RAW SMOKED HADDOCK	**95 (397)**
1 TABLESPOON CRÈME FRAÎCHE, 30% FAT	**30 (126)**
TOTAL	**587 (2456)**

Preparing my meal

Cook the lentils for the time indicated on the packet and let them cool (or rinse them under cold water to stop them cooking any further and then drain). Put the onion, coriander, lemon juice and zest in a bowl, and mix together. Add the mustard and olive oil, salt lightly, season with pepper and mix again. Add the lentils and combine. Taste and adjust the seasoning if necessary. Let the salad rest in the refrigerator before serving.

Second meal: as a change, add the raw smoked haddock chopped into small pieces.

Variation for men: add the tablespoon of crème fraîche at the same time as the mustard.

It's ready!

Veggie version: leave out the haddock and add more lentils.

120 G (4¼ OZ) LENTILS	**423 (1770)**
TOTAL	**498 (2084)**
VARIATION FOR MEN	
130 G (4½ OZ) LENTILS	**458 (1916)**
TOTAL	**563 (2356)**

NUTRITIONAL INFO

Lentils are an excellent source of protein for vegetarians and vegans. They are a good source of iron: about 7.5 mg per 100 g (3½ oz).

FISH & VEGETABLE
CURRY

Super
500

SERVES 1
PREPARATION TIME: 25 MINUTES
COOKING TIME: 40 MINUTES

INGREDIENTS	CAL (KJ)
½ ONION, ABOUT 50 G (1¾ OZ)	14 (59)
100 G (3½ OZ) TOMATOES	18 (75)
1 GARLIC CLOVE, CRUSHED	4 (17)
4 KAFFIR LIME LEAVES OR 1 LEMONGRASS STEM	2 (8)
2 CM (¾ IN) PIECE OF GINGER, GRATED	3 (13)
6 CORIANDER (CILANTRO) SPRIGS	2 (8)
1 TABLESPOON SOY SAUCE	10 (42)
1 TEASPOON CURRY POWDER	6 (25)
100 G (3½ OZ) GREEN BEANS	31 (130)
100 G (3½ OZ) BROCCOLI	34 (142)
100 G (3½ OZ) BABY ENGLISH SPINACH	24 (100)
50 G (1¾ OZ) BROWN BASMATI RICE	174 (728)
100 G (3½ OZ) COD, CUT INTO PIECES	80 (335)
100 G (3½ OZ) COOKED PRAWNS (SHRIMP), PEELED	80 (335)
½ TEASPOON BLACK SESAME SEEDS	13 (54)
TOTAL	**495 (2071)**

VARIATION FOR MEN	
70 G (2½ OZ) BROWN BASMATI RICE	244 (1021)
120 G (4¼ OZ) COD	96 (402)
120 G (4¼ OZ) COOKED PRAWNS (SHRIMP), PEELED	96 (402)
TOTAL	**597 (2498)**

Preparing my meal

Bring 500 ml (17 fl oz/2 cups) of water to the boil in a medium saucepan with the onion, tomato, garlic, kaffir lime leaves, ginger, coriander stems (set aside the leaves for later), soy sauce and curry powder. Season lightly with salt and pepper and cover. As soon as it comes to the boil, remove the lid and simmer gently for 30 minutes. Meanwhile, prepare the vegetables: wash and trim the beans, and wash the broccoli and baby spinach. Steam the green beans for 15 minutes; after 8 minutes of steaming time, add the broccoli. Purée the curry sauce, making sure to remove the kaffir lime leaves first. Cook the rice in a small saucepan of boiling salted water for the time indicated on the packet. Keep warm. Add the curry sauce to a deep frying pan or wok (thin out with a little boiling water if necessary). Add the vegetables, stir and heat gently for 2 minutes. Add the fish and the prawns, stir gently and cook for a further 3 minutes. Serve immediately sprinkled with chopped coriander leaves and sesame seeds, and accompanied by the rice.

It's ready!

Shopping: you can find kaffir lime leaves in the freezer section of Asian food stores. You can replace them with 1 lemongrass stem, cut into short lengths.

Tip: feel free to double the quantities on Non-Fast Days for a family meal or dinner with friends. In this case, slightly increase the amount of rice and add 100 ml (3½ fl oz) of coconut milk to the sauce.

NUTRITIONAL INFO
Sesame seeds are another super food and a rich source of omega-3 fatty acids.

FISH & BEAN SALAD,

COLD OR HOT!

Super **500**

SERVES 1

PREPARATION TIME: 15 MINUTES

COOKING TIME: 10 MINUTES

INGREDIENTS	CAL (KJ)
140 G (5 OZ) COOKED KIDNEY BEANS, OR 60 G (2¼ OZ) DRIED KIDNEY BEANS	204 (854)
90 G (3¼ OZ) COOKED CHICKPEAS, OR 25 G (1 OZ) DRIED CHICKPEAS	100 (418)
1 SMALL FENNEL BULB, ABOUT 150 G (5½ OZ)	47 (197)
2 BULB SPRING ONIONS (SCALLIONS), ABOUT 10 G (¼ OZ)	5 (21)
25 G (1 OZ/1 LARGE HANDFUL) ROCKET (ARUGULA), CHOPPED	6 (25)
12 CHERRY TOMATOES, ABOUT 150 G (5½ OZ/1 CUP), CHOPPED	24 (100)
2 FLAT-LEAF (ITALIAN) PARSLEY SPRIGS AND 2 TARRAGON SPRIGS, CHOPPED	2 (8)
1 TEASPOON HAZELNUT OIL	45 (188)
80 G (2¾ OZ) COD FILLET, OR OTHER FIRM WHITE FISH	64 (268)
TOTAL	**497 (2079)**

VARIATION FOR MEN	
1 LARGE EGG	90 (377)
TOTAL	**587 (2456)**

GLUTEN-FREE ◆

Preparing my meal

Rinse the kidney beans and chickpeas and put them in a bowl. Remove the hard outer layer of the fennel. Thinly slice the fennel and onions (bulbs and stems). Add the fennel and onions, the rocket, tomato and herbs to the beans and chickpeas. Dress with the hazelnut oil, salt and pepper.

First meal: steam the piece of fish for 6 minutes, cool and gently combine with a portion of salad.

Second meal: add 3 tablespoons of water to the salad and warm gently in a saucepan to eat hot.

Variation for men: add one soft-boiled egg (cooked for 5–6 minutes, then peeled under cold running water) to the hot version for dinner.

It's ready!

Tip: this salad is very hearty and nutritious; it is ideal for the early days of fasting. You can choose whether to eat the fish at lunch or dinner time …

Dried beans and chickpeas version: cook them according to the directions on the packet before using. Take note: the beans and chickpeas will need to be soaked for a few hours before cooking. See page 124 for instructions on cooking kidney beans.

'Speedy' version: use tinned kidney beans and chickpeas! There are some very good products available.

Veggie version: leave out the fish and add more kidney beans.

	CAL (KJ)
180 G (6¼ OZ) COOKED KIDNEY BEANS, OR 75 G (2½ OZ) DRIED	263 (1100)
TOTAL	**492 (2057)**
VARIATION FOR MEN	582 (2434)

PASTA
SALAD

Super
500

SERVES 1

PREPARATION TIME: 15 MINUTES

COOKING TIME: 10 MINUTES

INGREDIENTS	CAL (KJ)
100 G (3½ OZ) PASTA (OF YOUR CHOICE)	345 (1443)
8 CHERRY TOMATOES, ABOUT 100 G (3½ OZ)	18 (75)
1 TEASPOON OLIVE OIL	45 (188)
½ GARLIC CLOVE	2 (8)
ZEST AND JUICE OF ½ UNTREATED (ORGANIC) LIME	5 (21)
25 G (1 OZ/1 LARGE HANDFUL) ROCKET (ARUGULA), COARSELY CHOPPED	6 (25)
½ ZUCCHINI (COURGETTE), ABOUT 125 G (4½ OZ), DICED	21 (88)
30 G (1 OZ) CAPERBERRIES	8 (33)
3 BASIL SPRIGS	3 (13)
35 G (1¼ OZ) TINNED TUNA IN WATER, DRAINED AND FLAKED	41 (172)
TOTAL	**494 (2066)**

VARIATION FOR MEN	
120 G (4¼ OZ) PASTA (OF YOUR CHOICE)	414 (1732)
60 G (2¼ OZ) TINNED TUNA IN WATER, DRAINED AND FLAKED	69 (289)
TOTAL	**591 (2472)**

Preparing my meal

Cook the pasta according to the packet instructions until *al dente*. Run it immediately under cold water to stop it cooking further and drain. Purée half the tomatoes in a food processor with the olive oil, 2 tablespoons of water, the garlic, salt, pepper and lime juice. Pour the sauce over the pasta and toss. Add the rocket, the rest of the tomatoes (chopped), the zucchini, caperberries, lime zest and basil leaves. Mix again.

Second meal: add the tuna and mix it through.

It's ready!

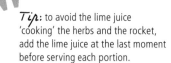

Tip: to avoid the lime juice 'cooking' the herbs and the rocket, add the lime juice at the last moment before serving each portion.

Shopping: if you can't find caperberries, use the smaller capers sold in jars.

Veggie version: leave out the tuna and add more pasta.

110 G (3¾ OZ) PASTA	380 (1590)
TOTAL	**488 (2041)**

VARIATION FOR MEN	
140 G (5 OZ) PASTA	483 (2021)
TOTAL	**591 (2472)**

NUTRITIONAL INFO

Consider using wholegrain or semi-wholegrain pasta. It doesn't affect the number of calories but it's more healthy: it has more fibre, vitamins and minerals.

CHICKEN, WITLOF,
LETTUCE & ARTICHOKES

Super
500

SERVES 1

PREPARATION TIME: 25 MINUTES

MARINATING TIME: 30 MINUTES

COOKING TIME: 11 MINUTES

INGREDIENTS	CAL (KJ)
JUICE OF ½ ORANGE, ABOUT 50 ML (1½ FL OZ)	23 (96)
1 TEASPOON OLIVE OIL	45 (188)
1 SMALL TEASPOON AGAVE SYRUP	16 (67)
180 G (6¼ OZ) CHICKEN BREAST FILLET	216 (904)
20 G (¾ OZ) COUSCOUS	75 (314)
150 G (5½ OZ) WITLOF (CHICORY)	26 (109)
1 SUCRINE (OR BABY COS) LETTUCE HEART	8 (33)
2 BULB SPRING ONIONS (SCALLIONS), ABOUT 10 G (¼ OZ)	5 (21)
4 COOKED ARTICHOKE HEARTS, ABOUT 100 G (3½ OZ), CHOPPED INTO SMALL PIECES	34 (142)
2 TARRAGON SPRIGS	2 (8)
1 TEASPOON HEMP SEEDS	33 (138)
GRATED ZEST OF ½ UNTREATED (ORGANIC) ORANGE	2 (8)
TOTAL	**485 (2028)**

VARIATION FOR MEN	
230 G (8¼ OZ) CHICKEN BREAST FILLET	276 (1155)
30 G (1 OZ) COUSCOUS	112 (469)
TOTAL	**582 (2434)**

Preparing my meal

Make a marinade from the orange juice, olive oil, agave syrup and a little salt and pepper. Cut the chicken breast in half horizontally and marinate it in the refrigerator for 30 minutes. Make the couscous as indicated on the packet, being careful not to overcook it and, above all, without adding oil or butter. Once cooked, fluff it up with a fork. Set aside. Clean and slice the witlof and lettuce into strips. Slice the onions (stems and bulbs). Drain the chicken breast (keep the marinade). Sear the chicken in a hot frying pan for 2 minutes on each side: it should be lightly browned. Slice the fillet into strips and set aside. In the same frying pan, brown half the witlof, lettuce and onions for 5 minutes over high heat, stirring occasionally. Add the artichoke hearts, tarragon, chicken, marinade and couscous, mix together and cook for a further 2 minutes. Transfer everything from the frying pan to a mixing bowl and add the rest of the vegetables. Mix together and serve sprinkled with hemp seeds and orange zest.

Second meal: warm gently in the pan, or it's also very good served cold.

It's ready!

Veggie version: leave out the chicken, add tofu and increase the quantity of couscous.

50 G (1¾ OZ) SMOKED TOFU (CUT INTO SMALL CUBES)	60 (251)
60 G (2¼ OZ) COUSCOUS	225 (941)
TOTAL	**479 (2004)**

VARIATION FOR MEN

50 G (1¾ OZ) SMOKED TOFU	60 (251)
90 G (3¼ OZ) COUSCOUS	336 (1406)
TOTAL	**590 (2467)**

Shopping: you can find hemp seeds in organic supermarkets. You can replace them with 1 teaspoon of sesame seeds (26 cal/109 kJ).

CHICKEN STIR-FRY

WITH BEAN SPROUTS

Super
500

SERVES 1

PREPARATION TIME: 20 MINUTES

COOKING TIME: 25 MINUTES

INGREDIENTS	CAL (KJ)
60 G (2¼ OZ/⅓ CUP) BURGHUL (BULGUR)	206 (862)
250 G (9 OZ) BEAN SPROUTS	75 (314)
150 G (5½ OZ) CHINESE CABBAGE (WONG BOK)	18 (75)
100 G (3½ OZ) CHICKEN BREAST FILLET	120 (502)
1 TEASPOON OLIVE OIL	45 (188)
1 CM (½ IN) PIECE OF GINGER, GRATED	2 (8)
1 SMALL FRENCH SHALLOT, CHOPPED	7 (29)
1 BULB SPRING ONION (SCALLION), BULB AND STEM THINLY SLICED	3 (13)
½ GARLIC CLOVE, CRUSHED	2 (8)
2 TABLESPOONS COCONUT WATER	5 (21)
1 TEASPOON SOY SAUCE	5 (21)
8 CORIANDER (CILANTRO) SPRIGS, CHOPPED	3 (13)
½ LIME, CUT INTO WEDGES	4 (17)
TOTAL	**495 (2071)**

VARIATION FOR MEN	
80 G (2¾ OZ) BURGHUL (BULGUR)	274 (1146)
130 G (4½ OZ) CHICKEN BREAST FILLET	156 (653)
TOTAL	**599 (2506)**

Preparing my meal

Cook the burghul in two and a half times its volume of boiling salted water, uncovered, on a medium heat, for 7 minutes. Let it stand off the heat for 5 minutes. Drain and set aside. Wash and drain the bean sprouts. Wash the cabbage leaves and slice them into fairly wide strips. Cut the chicken breast into small pieces. Add the olive oil to a hot wok, then sauté the chicken pieces with the ginger, shallot and onion for 2 minutes over high heat: all the pieces should be well browned on all sides. Add the garlic, cabbage, half the bean sprouts and 50 ml (1½ fl oz) of water. Continue cooking over medium heat for 8 minutes, stirring often. Once cooked, add the coconut water and soy sauce. Season lightly with salt and well with pepper, and mix together. Serve alongside the warmed burghul with the chopped coriander sprinkled on top. Add as many of the rest of the bean sprouts as you like, and serve with wedges of lime.

It's ready!

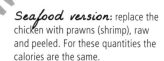

Seafood version: replace the chicken with prawns (shrimp), raw and peeled. For these quantities the calories are the same.

150 G (5½ OZ) PRAWNS	120 (502)
VARIATION FOR MEN	
195 G (6¾ OZ) PRAWNS	156 (653)

Tip: triple the quantities and this dish makes an ideal family meal for a Non-Fast Day!

NUTRITIONAL INFO

Bean sprouts are a good source of folate, essential for the synthesis of DNA and production of red blood cells.

VEAL
WITH PRESERVED LEMON

Super **500**

SERVES 1
PREPARATION TIME: 10 MINUTES
MARINATING TIME: 1 HOUR
COOKING TIME: 3 HOURS

INGREDIENTS	CAL (KJ)
½ PRESERVED LEMON	**9 (38)**
½ GARLIC CLOVE, CRUSHED	**2 (8)**
½ ONION, ABOUT 50 G (1¾ OZ), SLICED	**14 (59)**
8 CHERRY TOMATOES, ABOUT 100 G (3½ OZ), CUT INTO CUBES	**18 (75)**
30 G (1 OZ/2 LARGE HANDFULS) CORIANDER (CILANTRO) LEAVES, CHOPPED	**4 (17)**
JUICE OF 1 LEMON	**10 (42)**
1 TEASPOON OLIVE OIL	**45 (188)**
100 G (3½ OZ) VEAL TENDERLOIN, CUT INTO PIECES	**140 (586)**
50 G (1¾ OZ/⅓ CUP) SHELLED PEAS, OR 125 G (4½ OZ) IN THEIR PODS	**40 (167)**
50 G (1¾ OZ) COOKED ARTICHOKE HEARTS, CHOPPED	**17 (71)**
55 G (2 OZ) SPELT COUSCOUS	**188 (787)**
50 G (1¾ OZ) BABY ENGLISH SPINACH, WASHED	**12 (50)**
TOTAL	**499 (2088)**

VARIATION FOR MEN

120 G (4¼ OZ) VEAL TENDERLOIN, CUT INTO PIECES	**168 (703)**
75 G (2½ OZ) SPELT COUSCOUS	**257 (1075)**
TOTAL	**596 (2493)**

Preparing my meal

Rinse and slice the preserved lemon (remove seeds). In a small flameproof casserole dish, combine the garlic, onion, preserved lemon, tomato, half the coriander, the lemon juice, olive oil and pepper. Be careful not to add salt to this dish, as the preserved lemon already provides salt. Add the pieces of veal to this marinade, stir and marinate for 1 hour in the refrigerator. Preheat the oven to 150°C (300°F). Cover the meat with water, bring to the boil on the stovetop, then cover the casserole dish and bake in the oven for at least 3 hours. Check the dish occasionally, adding a little water if necessary. Fifteen minutes before the end of the cooking time, add the peas and the artichoke hearts. Cook the couscous in three times its volume of boiling salted water for 8 minutes over medium heat, then let it stand off the heat for 5 minutes. Serve the veal accompanied by the couscous, baby spinach and the rest of the coriander.

It's ready!

Fish version: replace the veal with sea bream, or another firm white fish.

140 G (5 OZ) SEA BREAM FILLET	**140 (586)**
TOTAL	**499 (2088)**
VARIATION FOR MEN	
165 G (5¾ OZ) SEA BREAM FILLET	**165 (690)**
TOTAL	**593 (2480)**

Method: cook the marinade in the casserole dish with 250 ml (9 fl oz/ 1 cup) of water in the oven for 1 hour. Add the vegetables and fish (cut into chunks) and cook for another 15 minutes. It's simpler, much faster and amazingly good.

Tip: this dish is also very good for Non-Fast Days. Increase the amount of meat a little and add other vegetables (carrots, turnips, etc.).

NUTRITIONAL INFO

Spelt is a very nutritious whole grain, which is perfect for Fast Days! It is a species of wheat, but since it has a lower gluten content than ordinary wheat, it can sometimes be tolerated by people who are sensitive to gluten.

LIKE A CHILLI

Super
500

SERVES 1

PREPARATION TIME: 15 MINUTES

COOKING TIME: 35 MINUTES

+ 45 MINUTES FOR RICE (MEN'S VERSION)

INGREDIENTS	CAL (KJ)
1 TEASPOON OLIVE OIL	45 (188)
½ RED ONION, CHOPPED	15 (63)
1 PINCH GROUND CUMIN	1 (4)
50 G (1¾ OZ) MINCED (GROUND) BEEF, 5% FAT	64 (268)
150 G (5½ OZ) TOMATOES	24 (100)
1 TEASPOON CHOPPED OREGANO	1 (4)
50 G (1¾ OZ) BABY ENGLISH SPINACH	12 (50)
1 PINCH CAYENNE PEPPER	1 (4)
1 GARLIC CLOVE, CHOPPED	4 (17)
330 G (11½ OZ) COOKED KIDNEY BEANS, OR 95 G (3¼ OZ) DRIED KIDNEY BEANS	323 (1351)
3 FLAT-LEAF (ITALIAN) PARSLEY SPRIGS, CHOPPED	2 (8)
TOTAL	**492 (2057)**

VARIATION FOR MEN

30 G (1 OZ) BROWN RICE	104 (435)
TOTAL	**596 (2492)**

GLUTEN-FREE ◆

Preparing my meal

Heat the olive oil in a small flameproof casserole dish. Add the onion and the cumin. Cook over medium heat for 5 minutes. Increase the heat, add the meat and brown it, breaking it up with a fork into little pieces. Be careful not to let it stew—the dish needs to be very hot so the meat sears. Add 100 ml (3½ fl oz) of water, the tomato, oregano, half the baby spinach (chopped), the cayenne pepper, garlic, salt and pepper. Let it cook on a low simmer for 15 minutes. Add the cooked beans and the parsley, cover and simmer for 10 minutes. At serving time, add the rest of the spinach and combine.

Variation for men: serve with brown rice. Pour the rice into two and a half times its volume of cold water in a saucepan. Add salt and simmer for 45 minutes over low heat.

It's ready!

On a personal note: my daughter Maë adores chilli. I double the quantities and we're set. I'm not all alone with my 'Super 500' and I make her happy.

Veggie version: leave out the minced beef and add (or increase for men's variation) the brown rice.

20 G (¾ OZ) BROWN RICE	69 (289)
TOTAL	**497 (2079)**
VARIATION FOR MEN	
45 G (1½ OZ) BROWN RICE	156 (653)
TOTAL	**584 (2443)**

Dried bean option: you can make this recipe using dried beans. See page 124 for full instructions on how to cook them properly.

NUTRITIONAL INFO

Can you eat spicy foods like chilli to lose weight? Some studies have found that capsaicin, a compound found in chillis, increases the feeling of fullness and stimulates the metabolism.

THAI VEGETABLE
SOUP

Super
500

SERVES 1

PREPARATION TIME: 25 MINUTES

COOKING TIME: 35 MINUTES

INGREDIENTS	CAL (KJ)
100 G (3½ OZ) THAI EGGPLANT (AUBERGINE)	24 (100)
100 G (3½ OZ) MUSHROOMS	22 (92)
100 G (3½ OZ) GREEN BEANS	31 (130)
100 G (3½ OZ) CHICKEN BREAST FILLET	120 (502)
5 G (⅛ OZ) PIECE OF GINGER, GRATED	4 (17)
½ GARLIC CLOVE, CRUSHED	2 (8)
750 ML (26 FL OZ/3 CUPS) CHICKEN STOCK, FAT REMOVED	12 (50)
1 TEASPOON RED CURRY PASTE	7 (29)
JUICE OF 1 LIME	8 (33)
4 KAFFIR LIME LEAVES	2 (8)
1 LEMONGRASS STEM, CUT INTO SHORT LENGTHS	2 (8)
40 G (1½ OZ/½ BUNCH) CORIANDER (CILANTRO), CHOPPED	5 (21)
8 CHERRY TOMATOES, ABOUT 100 G (3½ OZ)	18 (75)
55 G (2 OZ) CELLOPHANE NOODLES	183 (766)
50 G (1¾ OZ) BEAN SPROUTS	15 (63)
1 TEASPOON SESAME OIL	45 (188)
TOTAL	**500 (2090)**

VARIATION FOR MEN	
140 G (5 OZ) CHICKEN BREAST FILLET	168 (703)
70 G (2½ OZ) CELLOPHANE NOODLES	233 (975)
TOTAL	**598 (2502)**

Preparing my meal

Wash and prepare all the vegetables: quarter the eggplant, chop the mushrooms into pieces and cut the green beans into long sections. Cut the chicken breast into cubes. Heat a frying pan and brown the chicken over high heat for 5 minutes with the ginger and garlic. Be careful not to let it burn, and reduce the heat if necessary. Keep the chicken warm. Heat the chicken stock with the red curry paste, lime juice, kaffir lime leaves and lemongrass, and bring to the boil. Add the eggplant, chicken, green beans and half the coriander. Lower the heat and simmer for 20 minutes. Before serving, add the mushrooms, tomatoes, noodles and bean sprouts, and cook for another 5 minutes. Dress with a little sesame oil and scatter over the rest of the coriander before serving.

It's ready!

Veggie version: leave out the chicken and increase the quantity of noodles.

90 G (3¼ OZ) CELLOPHANE NOODLES	299 (1251)
TOTAL	**496 (2075)**

VARIATION FOR MEN	
120 G (4¼ OZ) CELLOPHANE NOODLES	399 (1669)
TOTAL	**596 (2493)**

My advice: for best results, I suggest setting aside half the tomatoes, noodles and bean sprouts for the second meal, and cooking them when reheating the soup.

Shopping: if you go to an Asian food store, buy a few leaves of Thai basil, whose aroma and flavour will work beautifully with this delicious soup. If you can't find Thai eggplant, use 100 g (3½ oz) of regular eggplant, cut into large cubes.

Kaffir lime leaves are sold in Asian stores in the freezer section. Replace the lime leaves with an extra lemongrass stem if you can't get them.

BEEF & CARROTS

Super 500

SERVES 1

PREPARATION TIME: 10 MINUTES

COOKING TIME: 3 HOURS

INGREDIENTS	CAL (KJ)
100 G (3½ OZ) BEEF ROUND OR RUMP STEAK, CUT INTO PIECES	160 (669)
250 G (9 OZ) CARROTS, CUT INTO LARGE PIECES	103 (431)
2 SMALL FRENCH SHALLOTS	15 (63)
GRATED ZEST OF ½ UNTREATED (ORGANIC) ORANGE	2 (8)
½ TEASPOON FENNEL SEEDS	3 (13)
60 G (2¼ OZ) BROWN BASMATI RICE	207 (866)
2 FLAT-LEAF (ITALIAN) PARSLEY SPRIGS, CHOPPED	2 (8)
25 G (1 OZ/1 LARGE HANDFUL) ROCKET (ARUGULA)	6 (25)
TOTAL	**498 (2083)**

VARIATION FOR MEN	
140 G (5 OZ) BEEF ROUND STEAK, CUT INTO PIECES	224 (937)
70 G (2½ OZ) BROWN BASMATI RICE	244 (1021)
TOTAL	**599 (2506)**

GLUTEN-FREE ◆

Preparing my meal

Put the meat in a small flameproof casserole dish with the carrots, shallots, orange zest, fennel seeds and salt and pepper. Preheat the oven to 150°C (300°F). Cover the meat with water and bring to the boil on the stovetop, then cover and bake in the oven for at least 3 hours. Cook the rice in a small saucepan of boiling salted water, uncovered, for 11 minutes over medium heat. Serve the beef and carrots sprinkled with parsley and accompanied by the rice, broth and rocket.

It's ready!

Variation: replace the zest of the ½ orange with the zest of 1 untreated (organic) lemon.

Tip: this dish is also very good for Non-Fast Days. Add some roasting potatoes and slightly increase the amount of meat.

On a personal note: Oops! Some friends ask themselves over to dinner on a day I want to be a Fast Day. No problem! I double or triple the quantities and make sure that I don't take more than my share.

NUTRITIONAL INFO

Beef is an excellent source of vitamin B and zinc, which play a role in maintaining a healthy immune system. Lean beef is surprisingly low in fat. You can take advantage of it on your Fast Days!

RED RICE
WITH CAULIFLOWER & SPROUTS

SERVES 1
PREPARATION TIME: 20 MINUTES
COOKING TIME: 45 MINUTES

INGREDIENTS	CAL (KJ)
80 G (2¾ OZ) RED RICE	290 (1213)
50 G (1¾ OZ) CHICKEN BREAST FILLET	60 (251)
100 G (3½ OZ) CAULIFLOWER	25 (105)
JUICE OF 1 LEMON, ABOUT 25 ML (¾ FL OZ)	10 (42)
1 TEASPOON OLIVE OIL	45 (188)
1 TEASPOON CANOLA OIL	45 (188)
50 G (1¾ OZ) SPROUTS (EG, CABBAGE OR ALFALFA)	14 (59)
2 BULB SPRING ONIONS (SCALLIONS), BULB AND STEM THINLY SLICED	5 (21)
4 MINT SPRIGS AND 4 PARSLEY SPRIGS, CHOPPED	4 (17)
TOTAL	**498 (2084)**

VARIATION FOR MEN	
105 G (3½ OZ/½ CUP) RED RICE	381 (1594)
TOTAL	**589 (2465)**

GLUTEN-FREE ◆

Preparing my meal

Pour the rice into a medium saucepan with three times its volume of cold water. Add salt and cook for 45 minutes on a low simmer. Let the rice cool or stop it cooking any further by rinsing it under cold water, then drain. Meanwhile, steam the chicken for 10 minutes. Let it cool and cut into small cubes. Prepare the cauliflower: using a mandoline, shred the top of the florets to make a 'cauliflower rice'. In a bowl, combine the lemon juice with the oils and two or three turns of the pepper mill. Add the chicken, the cauliflower rice, the sprouts, onions and herbs. Mix well and place in the refrigerator. When serving, taste and adjust the salt and pepper if necessary.

It's ready!

Tip: to stop the lemon juice 'cooking' the herbs, add them at the last minute.

Shopping: you'll find red rice in organic food stores.

Veggie version:
Leave out the chicken and increase the quantity of red rice.

95 G (3¼ OZ) RED RICE	344 (1439)
TOTAL	**492 (2059)**
VARIATION FOR MEN	
120 G (4¼ OZ) RED RICE	435 (1820)
TOTAL	**583 (2439)**

NUTRITIONAL INFO

Cauliflower, a member of the Brassicaceae family, is a real super food. This family of vegetables contains phytonutrients called glucosinolates, which help optimise liver function and support the body's natural detoxification cycles.

CHARLOTTE'S
PILAF

SERVES 1

PREPARATION TIME: 15 MINUTES

COOKING TIME: 1 HOUR

INGREDIENTS	CAL (KJ)
80 G (2¾ OZ) BUTTERNUT PUMPKIN (SQUASH)	40 (167)
½ RED ONION	15 (63)
100 G (3½ OZ) FENNEL BULB	31 (130)
½ RED CAPSICUM (PEPPER), ABOUT 125 G (4½ OZ)	31 (130)
1 TEASPOON OLIVE OIL	45 (188)
1 SMALL CHICKEN THIGH, ABOUT 100 G (3½ OZ)	95 (397)
1 GARLIC CLOVE	4 (17)
50 G (1¾ OZ) MILLET	189 (791)
1 TEASPOON BALSAMIC VINEGAR	2 (8)
2 BASIL SPRIGS, CHOPPED	2 (8)
4 CHIVES, SNIPPED	1 (4)
50 G (1¾ OZ/2 LARGE HANDFULS) ENGLISH SPINACH OR ROCKET (ARUGULA)	12 (50)
5 G (⅛ OZ) FRESHLY GRATED PARMESAN CHEESE	22 (92)
TOTAL	489 (2045)

VARIATION FOR MEN	
70 G (2½ OZ/⅓ CUP) MILLET	265 (1109)
10 G (¼ OZ) GRATED PARMESAN CHEESE	44 (184)
TOTAL	587 (2455)

GLUTEN-FREE ◆

Preparing my meal

Preheat the oven to 200°C (400°F). Cut the pumpkin and onion into cubes. Remove the hard outer layer of the fennel. Wash the capsicum and fennel and cut into pieces. Put all the vegetables in a baking dish, add 2 drops of the olive oil, salt and pepper, stir together and cook in the oven for 15 minutes, stirring occasionally. Add the chicken thigh and garlic, and cook for another 45 minutes. Meanwhile, put the millet in a medium saucepan with a large quantity of salted water, and cook for 15 minutes. Run the millet under cold water to stop it cooking any further and drain. Remove the garlic from the baking dish, peel it and crush it. Make the dressing by mixing the garlic with the rest of the olive oil, the balsamic vinegar, salt and pepper and 1 teaspoon of water. Pull the chicken thigh apart to remove the skin, fat and bones, and cut the flesh into small pieces. Combine the millet with the vegetables and herbs. Dress the salad with the sauce.

First meal: add the chicken and half the salad.

Second meal: add the grated parmesan and the other half of the salad.

It's ready!

Variation: replace the millet with brown basmati rice.

50 G (1¾ OZ) BASMATI RICE	175 (732)
TOTAL	475 (1986)
VARIATION FOR MEN	
75 G (2½ OZ) BASMATI RICE	262 (1096)
TOTAL	584 (2442)

On a personal note: thanks to Charlotte 'the redhead' for this delicious recipe, original and complete!

NUTRITIONAL INFO

Millet is not just for the birds. This little seed is high in protein and magnesium, with a taste that's similar to hazelnut.

Chapter 2

À LA CARTE RECIPES

CRISPY
WITLOF

103 *calories*

SERVES 1
PREPARATION TIME: 10 MINUTES
COOKING TIME: 10 MINUTES

INGREDIENTS	CAL (KJ)
2 WITLOF (CHICORIES), ABOUT 200 G (7 OZ)	34 (142)
2 BASIL SPRIGS	2 (8)
1 FLAT-LEAF (ITALIAN) PARSLEY SPRIG	1 (4)
2 TABLESPOONS LEMON JUICE	6 (25)
1 SMALL TEASPOON AGAVE SYRUP	16 (67)
10 G (¼ OZ) FRESHLY GRATED PARMESAN CHEESE	44 (184)
TOTAL	**103 (430)**

GLUTEN-FREE ◆

Preparing my meal

Cut the witlof in half lengthways. Remove the basil and parsley leaves from the stems and slip them between the witlof leaves. Heat the oven grill (broiler). Put the witlof in a baking dish and sprinkle with the lemon juice, agave syrup, half the parmesan cheese, salt and pepper. Slide under the grill (not too close) and cook for 10 minutes to make them nice and crispy. Make sure they don't burn—move them away from the grill or put some foil on top as soon as they are golden brown. Serve with the remaining parmesan cheese.

It's ready!

Extra: For a more complete meal, serve with grilled meat or steamed pollack. Alternatively, try cod or john dory.

MEAT	
100 G (3½ OZ) GRILLED STEAK	136 (569)
TOTAL	239 (999)

FISH	
120 G (4¼ OZ) POLLACK	108 (452)
TOTAL	211 (882)

TOMATO TART

197 *calories*

SERVES 1

PREPARATION TIME: 15 MINUTES

COOKING TIME: 10 MINUTES

INGREDIENTS	CAL (KJ)
40 G (1½ OZ) PUFF PASTRY, FROM ROLL OF PUFF PASTRY	152 (636)
16 CHERRY TOMATOES, ABOUT 200 G (7 OZ)	36 (151)
½ TEASPOON MUSTARD	3 (13)
½ TEASPOON TOMATO PASTE (CONCENTRATED PURÉE)	5 (21)
1 BASIL SPRIG	1 (4)
TOTAL	197 (825)

Preparing my meal

Cut a 14 cm (5½ in) circle from the roll of pastry and keep the rest of the pastry for the family, friends, next time … Place the pastry base on some baking paper, prick with a fork and place in the refrigerator. Preheat the oven to 210°C (410°F). Wash the tomatoes and slice them into thin rounds. Mix together the mustard and tomato paste. Retrieve the pastry base from the refrigerator and spread the mustard/tomato mix over the base, with the tomato slices arranged on top. Season with salt and pepper, and cook for 10 minutes in the middle of the oven. At serving time, scatter over the basil leaves.

It's ready!

Note: choose the lightest possible pastry (the calories will be shown on the packet). Don't go above 400 calories (1674 kilojoules) per 100 g (3½ oz) of pastry.

Variation: you can add a big handful of rocket.

25 G (1 OZ/1 LARGE HANDFUL) ROCKET (ARUGULA)	6 (25)
TOTAL	203 (850)

CRISP
& TANGY SALAD

87 *calories*

SERVES 1

PREPARATION TIME: 10 MINUTES

INGREDIENTS	CAL (KJ)
3 SUCRINE (OR BABY COS) LETTUCES	23 (96)
1 BASIL SPRIG	1 (4)
⅓ PRESERVED LEMON	7 (29)
⅓ TEASPOON GROUND CUMIN	2 (8)
4 CHERRY TOMATOES, ABOUT 50 G (1¾ OZ)	9 (38)
1 TEASPOON OLIVE OIL	45 (188)
TOTAL	87 (363)

GLUTEN-FREE ◆

Preparing my meal

Wash and chop the lettuce leaves to make a salad. Remove the basil leaves from the stem, and set aside. Rinse the preserved lemon under cold running water and remove the seeds. Add the preserved lemon, cumin, tomato, olive oil and pepper to the bowl of a food processor. Purée together and pour over the salad. Add the basil leaves, toss and serve.

It's ready!

Extra: add some chicken, steamed for 15 minutes and thinly sliced, or some cooked prawns.

CHICKEN	
120 G (4½ OZ) CHICKEN	144 (602)
TOTAL	231 (965)

PRAWNS	
100 G (3½ OZ) COOKED PRAWNS (SHRIMP)	80 (335)
TOTAL	167 (698)

FRUITY
GRATED CARROTS

86 *calories*

SERVES 1

PREPARATION TIME: 10 MINUTES

INGREDIENTS	CAL (KJ)
150 G (5½ OZ) CARROTS	62 (259)
1 TEASPOON LEMON JUICE	2 (8)
1 TABLESPOON FRESHLY SQUEEZED ORANGE JUICE	2 (8)
1 SMALL TEASPOON AGAVE SYRUP	16 (67)
1 TEASPOON WHITE WINE VINEGAR	2 (8)
5 CORIANDER (CILANTRO) SPRIGS, LEAVES CHOPPED	2 (8)
TOTAL	86 (358)

GLUTEN-FREE ◆

Preparing my meal

Grate the carrots on the coarsest grater setting. Make a vinaigrette by combining the lemon juice, orange juice, agave syrup, vinegar, salt and pepper, and mix it with the carrots. Let the salad stand for at least 1 hour in the refrigerator before eating; it will be tastier and juicier. At the last minute, scatter over the coriander.

Sweet and sour variation: add grated mango to the mixture.

50 G (1¾ OZ) MANGO	32 (134)
TOTAL	118 (492)

Extra: add toasted and crushed hazelnuts to the salad at the last minute.

WITHOUT MANGO

10 G (¼ OZ) HAZELNUTS	63 (264)
TOTAL	149 (622)

WITH MANGO

10 G (¼ OZ) HAZELNUTS	63 (264)
50 G (1¾ OZ) MANGO	32 (134)
TOTAL	181 (756)

SPRING
ASPARAGUS

85 *calories*

SERVES 1
PREPARATION TIME: 15 MINUTES
COOKING TIME: 15 MINUTES

INGREDIENTS	CAL (KJ)
150 G (5½ OZ) WHITE ASPARAGUS	**36 (151)**
1 TEASPOON LEMON JUICE	**2 (8)**
1 TEASPOON OLIVE OIL	**45 (188)**
FLEUR DE SEL (FINE SEA SALT)	
10 CHIVES, SNIPPED	**2 (8)**
TOTAL	**85 (355)**

GLUTEN-FREE ◆

Preparing my meal

Trim the base of the asparagus spears, then peel them without touching the tip—this would be a sacrilege because it's the best part! Rinse them under cold water and steam for 10–15 minutes, depending on their size. Make the vinaigrette: mix the lemon juice, olive oil, 1 teaspoon water, sea salt and freshly ground black pepper. Check whether the asparagus spears are cooked by inserting the tip of a knife into one of the spears. Let them cool until just warm and serve immediately, sprinkled with chives and accompanied by the vinaigrette.

It's ready!

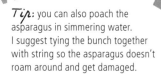

Tip: you can also poach the asparagus in simmering water. I suggest tying the bunch together with string so the asparagus doesn't roam around and get damaged.

Extra: add some freshly grated parmesan cheese. There are these extraordinary Microplane® graters available that grate very finely, creating very light grated foods.

5 G (⅛ OZ) PARMESAN CHEESE	**22 (92)**
TOTAL	**107 (447)**

Extra: serve with cod or other firm white fish, steamed for 10 minutes, and some quinoa. See page 124 for how to cook quinoa.

100 G (3½ OZ) COD	**80 (335)**
85 G (3 OZ) COOKED QUINOA	**147 (615)**
OR 40 G (1½ OZ) RAW	
TOTAL	**312 (1305)**

STEAMED
HEIRLOOM VEGETABLES

117 *calories*

SERVES 1
PREPARATION TIME: 15 MINUTES
COOKING TIME: 20 MINUTES

INGREDIENTS	CAL (KJ)
50 G (1¾ OZ) JERUSALEM ARTICHOKES	37 (155)
50 G (1¾ OZ) TURNIP (COLOURED ONES ARE PRETTIER)	15 (63)
50 G (1¾ OZ) BLACK RADISH ALTERNATIVELY, USE SWEDE (RUTABAGA)	10 (42)
50 G (1¾ OZ) PARSNIP	38 (159)
20 G (¾ OZ) RAW BEETROOT (BEETS)	5 (21)
½ TEASPOON CHIA SEEDS	10 (42)
5 CHERVIL SPRIGS, CHOPPED	2 (8)
TOTAL	**117 (490)**

GLUTEN-FREE ◆

Preparing my meal

Wash, peel and cut the Jerusalem artichokes, turnip, black radish and parsnip into pieces the same size. Steam them for 20 minutes. As soon as they are cooked, transfer them to a plate. Grate the beetroot over the top, salt lightly and season with pepper, sprinkle with chia seeds and scatter over the chervil.

It's ready!

Extra: for a more complete meal, serve with quinoa (see page 124 for how to cook quinoa) and bresaola.

75 G (2½ OZ) COOKED QUINOA	128 (536)
OR 35 G (1¼ OZ) RAW	
3 SLICES (24 G/1 OZ) BRESAOLA	36 (151)
(ALTERNATIVELY, USE BEEF JERKY OR OTHER DRIED MEAT)	
TOTAL	**281 (1177)**

Tip: if you choose organic vegetables (like I do), you won't need to peel the radish, turnip and parsnip after rinsing them under water.

NUTRITIONAL INFO

Chia seeds are very good for you and are part of the family of foods rich in omega-3 fatty acids. You'll find them in organic food shops.

BOWL
OF PASTA

324 *calories*

SERVES 1
PREPARATION TIME: 15 MINUTES
COOKING TIME: 10 MINUTES

INGREDIENTS	CAL (KJ)
75 G (2½ OZ) WHEAT PASTA	258 (1079)
100 G (3½ OZ) TOMATOES	18 (75)
5 ROCKET (ARUGULA) LEAVES	2 (8)
½ TEASPOON OLIVE OIL	23 (96)
1 BASIL SPRIG, LEAVES PICKED	1 (4)
5 G (⅛ OZ) FRESHLY GRATED PARMESAN CHEESE	22 (92)
TOTAL	324 (1354)

Preparing my meal

Cook the pasta until it's *al dente* so its glycaemic index isn't too high, because the more pasta is cooked, the faster its carbohydrates are released! Purée the tomatoes in a blender with the rocket, olive oil and a little salt and pepper. Heat this sauce for a few minutes in a saucepan over medium heat and pour it over the pasta as soon as it is cooked. Scatter over the basil leaves and the parmesan.

It's ready!

On a personal note: like the tomato tart, this recipe 'costs' a lot of calories for its serving size! But it's good to give yourself a 'different' kind of indulgence from time to time.

Extra: add some tinned tuna in water or cooked minced beef to the sauce when heating it up.

TUNA	
25 G (1 OZ) TUNA IN WATER, DRAINED	29 (121)
TOTAL	353 (1475)

BEEF	
25 G (1 OZ) MINCED (GROUND) BEEF (5% FAT)	34 (142)
TOTAL	358 (1496)

STEAMED BROCCOLI
& SOY SAUCE

66 calories

SERVES 1

PREPARATION TIME: 5 MINUTES

COOKING TIME: 7 MINUTES

INGREDIENTS	CAL (KJ)
130 G (4½ OZ) BROCCOLI FLORETS, WASHED	44 (184)
1 TABLESPOON RICE VINEGAR	4 (17)
1 TEASPOON SOY SAUCE	5 (21)
½ TEASPOON SESAME SEEDS	13 (54)
TOTAL	**66 (276)**

Preparing my meal

Steam the broccoli florets for 7 minutes, then stop them cooking any further by dropping them into iced water. Drain and let them dry on paper towel. Meanwhile, make the dressing by mixing the rice vinegar, soy sauce and some pepper. Serve the broccoli sprinkled with sesame seeds and the dressing.

It's ready!

Variation: sprinkle the broccoli (hot or cold) with olive oil and freshly grated parmesan cheese.

1 TEASPOON OLIVE OIL	45 (188)
5 G (⅛ OZ) PARMESAN CHEESE	22 (92)
TOTAL	**133 (556)**

GREEN SALAD

WITH HERBS, PURE & SIMPLE

66 *calories*

SERVES 1

PREPARATION TIME: 10 MINUTES

INGREDIENTS	CAL (KJ)
25 G (1 OZ/1 LARGE HANDFUL) MIXED SALAD LEAVES	7 (29)
2 CORIANDER (CILANTRO) SPRIGS	2 (8)
2 CHERVIL SPRIGS	1 (4)
1 TARRAGON SPRIG	1 (4)
1 BASIL SPRIG	1 (4)
1 MINT SPRIG	1 (4)
1 TEASPOON SOY SAUCE	5 (21)
1 TEASPOON LIME JUICE	2 (8)
1 TEASPOON OLIVE OIL	45 (188)
½ TEASPOON GRATED ZEST FROM UNTREATED (ORGANIC) LIME	1 (4)
TOTAL	66 (274)

Preparing my meal

Wash and dry the salad leaves. Wash all the fresh herbs and pluck off the leaves. Make the dressing: mix the soy sauce, lime juice, olive oil, 1 teaspoon of water and freshly ground black pepper. Combine the salad leaves and herbs and add the dressing. Combine and sprinkle with lime zest before eating.

It's ready!

This is the salad that goes with everything:

100 g (3½ oz) beef tenderloin (150 cal/628 kJ), seared briefly for 1 minute on each side, thinly sliced and sprinkled with 5 g (⅛ oz) freshly grated parmesan cheese (22 cal/92 kJ) and covered with salad.
TOTAL 238 (994)

100 g (3½ oz) cod fillet (80 cal/ 335 kJ), or another firm white fish, steamed for 10–12 minutes.
TOTAL 146 (609)

1 large soft-boiled egg (90 cal/377 kJ), cooked for 5–6 minutes in boiling water, peeled under cold running water and broken on top of the salad.
TOTAL 156 (651)

100 g (3½ oz) cooked prawns (shrimp) (80 cal/335 kJ), peeled. Combine with the salad and add a 1 cm (½ in) piece of ginger, grated (2 cal/8 kJ).
TOTAL 148 (617)

100 g (3½ oz) chicken breast (120 cal/502 kJ), browned for 2 minutes each side in a frying pan over medium–high heat, then cooked for a further 5 minutes, covered, over low heat.
TOTAL 186 (776)

LEEKS
& LICORICE ROOT

202 *calories*

SERVES 1

PREPARATION TIME: 10 MINUTES

COOKING TIME: 10 MINUTES

INGREDIENTS	CAL (KJ)
150 G (5½ OZ) LEEK	84 (351)
1 MEDIUM EGG, ABOUT 60 G (2¼ OZ)	71 (297)
1 TEASPOON OLIVE OIL	45 (188)
FLEUR DE SEL (FINE SEA SALT)	
1 STICK LICORICE ROOT	2 (8)
TOTAL	**202 (844)**

GLUTEN-FREE ◆

Preparing my meal

Prepare the leek: cut off the root end and the top of the green section (about two-thirds) and slice completely through lengthways to wash thoroughly. Steam for 10 minutes. Meanwhile, cook the egg for 5–6 minutes in boiling water, then peel it under cold running water. Serve the leeks lukewarm, drizzled with a little olive oil and sprinkled with sea salt and freshly ground pepper. Grate the licorice root over the top and add the soft-boiled egg.

It's ready!

Variations: replace the leeks with alternative vegetables.

200 G (7 OZ) GREEN BEANS, STEAMED FOR 10–15 MINUTES	62 (259)
TOTAL	**180 (752)**
200 G (7 OZ) BROCCOLI, STEAMED FOR 7 MINUTES	64 (268)
TOTAL	**182 (761)**
150 G (5½ OZ) PEAS, STEAMED FOR 10–15 MINUTES	120 (502)
TOTAL	**238 (995)**

Extra light version: leave out the egg.

TOTAL	**131 (547)**

Tip: if you don't like licorice, replace it with a pinch of vanilla powder, cumin, Espelette pepper, chilli powder, curry powder … The choice is yours!

Shopping: you can find a stick of licorice root at a pharmacy or online. I use my 'magic' Microplane® grater to make a licorice powder. I don't add too much and it's delicious!

GRILLED
GREEN BEANS

126 calories

SERVES 1

PREPARATION TIME: 10 MINUTES

COOKING TIME: 20 MINUTES

INGREDIENTS	CAL (KJ)
150 G (5½ OZ) GREEN BEANS	47 (197)
1 TEASPOON OLIVE OIL	45 (188)
8 CHERRY TOMATOES, ABOUT 100 G (3½ OZ), CHOPPED	18 (75)
½ ONION, ABOUT 50 G (1¾ OZ), THINLY SLICED	14 (59)
3 FLAT-LEAF (ITALIAN) PARSLEY SPRIGS, CHOPPED	2 (8)
TOTAL	**126 (527)**

GLUTEN-FREE ◆

Preparing my meal

Cook the green beans in a large quantity of boiling salted water for 10 minutes. Drain and dry well. Heat the olive oil in a large frying pan, add the beans, tomato and onion, and cook over medium heat for 10 minutes, stirring occasionally. Season with salt and pepper and scatter over the parsley at serving time.

It's ready!

On a personal note: it's not necessarily good for you, but if you let the vegetables burn a little, it produces a slightly charred flavour that is really delicious. In the end, it's a question of taste!

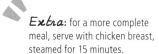

Extra: for a more complete meal, serve with chicken breast, steamed for 15 minutes.

1 CHICKEN BREAST FILLET, ABOUT 120 G (4¼ OZ)	144 (602)
TOTAL	**270 (1129)**

DIP
& CRUDITÉS

206 *calories*

SERVES 1

PREPARATION TIME: 15 MINUTES

INGREDIENTS	CAL (KJ)
75 G (2½ OZ) TINNED TUNA IN WATER, DRAINED	87 (364)
3 TABLESPOONS PLAIN YOGHURT, 20% FAT	21 (88)
2 TEASPOONS CAPERS, ABOUT 8 G (¼ OZ)	2 (8)
6 CHIVES, SNIPPED	2 (8)
2 BASIL SPRIGS, CHOPPED	2 (8)
6 WITLOF (CHICORY) LEAVES, ABOUT 50 G (1¾ OZ)	9 (38)
½ CUCUMBER, ABOUT 200 G (7 OZ)	24 (100)
8 CHERRY TOMATOES, ABOUT 100 G (3½ OZ)	18 (75)
1 CARROT, ABOUT 100 G (3½ OZ)	41 (172)
DIP TOTAL	**114 (476)**
VEGETABLE TOTAL	**92 (385)**
TOTAL	**206 (861)**

GLUTEN-FREE ◆

Preparing my meal

Make the dip: flake the tuna with a fork and add the yoghurt, capers, chives, basil, and salt and pepper. Set aside in the refrigerator. Prepare the vegetables: wash the witlof leaves, cucumber and tomatoes, peel the carrot and cut the cucumber into sticks.

It's ready!

Seasonal variation: you can give variety to this dish by using different vegetables. Add 100 g (3½ oz) of the following alternatives:

- black radish (20 cal/84 kJ)
- fennel (31 cal/130 kJ)
- raw zucchini (courgette) (17 cal/71 kJ)
- cauliflower (25 cal/105 kJ)

Dip variation 1: add 1 teaspoon of mustard (5 cal/21 kJ) and 1 pinch of curry powder (1 cal/4 kJ).

DIP TOTAL 120 (501)

Dip variation 2: add the juice and grated zest of ½ lime (5 cal/21 kJ) and a 5 mm (¼ in) piece of ginger, grated (1 cal/4 kJ).

DIP TOTAL 120 (501)

INDIAN-STYLE
SPINACH

172 *calories*

SERVES 1
PREPARATION TIME: 15 MINUTES
COOKING TIME: 17 MINUTES

INGREDIENTS	CAL (KJ)
300 G (10½ OZ) ENGLISH SPINACH	70 (293)
½ ONION, ABOUT 50 G (1¾ OZ), SLICED	14 (59)
½ TEASPOON GROUND CUMIN	2 (8)
1 CARDAMOM SEED	1 (4)
½ TEASPOON GROUND CINNAMON	3 (13)
1 BAY LEAF	1 (4)
1 CLOVE	1 (4)
1 MEDIUM TOMATO, ABOUT 100 G (3½ OZ), COARSELY CHOPPED	18 (75)
½ GARLIC CLOVE, CRUSHED	2 (8)
1 CM (½ IN) PIECE OF GINGER, GRATED	2 (8)
½ TEASPOON GROUND TURMERIC	2 (8)
1 TABLESPOON TOMATO SAUCE (KETCHUP)	10 (42)
25 ML (¾ FL OZ) SOY CREAM (FOR COOKING)	43 (180)
6 CORIANDER (CILANTRO) SPRIGS, CHOPPED	3 (13)
TOTAL	**172 (719)**

GLUTEN-FREE ◆

Preparing my meal

Pick over the spinach, removing the stems and any damaged leaves. Wash and drain, then chop it coarsely. Heat a wok or large frying pan over medium heat, add the onion, cumin, cardamom, cinnamon, bay leaf, clove, tomato, garlic and ginger. Cook, stirring, for 2 minutes. Add the spinach, stir and cook over high heat for 3 minutes, then over medium heat for 7 minutes until it turns a dark green. Sprinkle with turmeric and stir in the tomato sauce and soy cream. Cook over medium heat, stirring, for 5 minutes. Before serving, scatter over the coriander. Taste and adjust the salt and pepper if necessary.

It's ready!

Extra: serve with pollack, steamed for 10 minutes. Alternatively, try cod or john dory.

120 G (4¼ OZ) POLLACK	108 (452)
TOTAL	**280 (1171)**

ARTICHOKE
WITH THAI VINAIGRETTE

133 *calories*

SERVES 1

PREPARATION TIME: 10 MINUTES

COOKING TIME: 30 MINUTES

INGREDIENTS	CAL (KJ)
1 BRETON (OR GLOBE) ARTICHOKE	76 (318)
1 TEASPOON OLIVE OIL	45 (188)
1 TEASPOON SOY SAUCE	5 (21)
½ TEASPOON GRATED GINGER	2 (8)
2 TEASPOONS COCONUT WATER	2 (8)
⅓ SMALL FRENCH SHALLOT, CHOPPED	2 (8)
1 CORIANDER (CILANTRO) SPRIG, CHOPPED	1 (4)
TOTAL	**133 (555)**

Preparing my meal

Cook the artichoke in simmering salted water for about 30 minutes; it is cooked when one of the outer leaves can be detached easily. Drain and allow to cool until lukewarm. My technique for making vinaigrette: put the olive oil, soy sauce, ginger, coconut water, shallot, coriander and pepper into a jam jar. Shake and it's ready! Pull off the artichoke leaves as you eat, starting from the outside, and dunk them into the sauce. Then extricate the heart of the artichoke, remove the 'choke' and pour over the rest of the dressing.

It's ready!

Tip: you can also cook the artichoke in a pressure cooker. In that case, allow 10 minutes simmering time or 12 minutes steaming time from when the pressure valve starts to rotate.

Extra: serve with a prawn (shrimp) and baby spinach salad dressed with 1 teaspoon olive oil, salt and pepper.

100 G (3½ OZ) COOKED PRAWNS (SHRIMP)	80 (335)
25 G (1 OZ/1 HANDFUL) BABY ENGLISH SPINACH	6 (25)
1 TEASPOON OLIVE OIL	45 (188)
TOTAL	**264 (1103)**

Vinaigrette variation: for a more traditional vinaigrette, mix together olive oil, white wine vinegar, mustard and salt and pepper. Thin out with 1 teaspoon of water if necessary.

1 TEASPOON OLIVE OIL	45 (188)
½ TEASPOON VINEGAR	1 (4)
½ TEASPOON MUSTARD	3 (13)
TOTAL	**125 (523)**

Green version: replace the artichoke with broccoli, steamed for 7 minutes, and serve with the Thai vinaigrette and sesame seeds.

120 G (4¼ OZ) BROCCOLI	41 (172)
½ TEASPOON SESAME SEEDS	13 (54)
THAI VINAIGRETTE	57 (238)
TOTAL	**111 (464)**

MISO SOUP
REVISITED

33 calories

SERVES 1
PREPARATION TIME: 15 MINUTES
COOKING TIME: 10 MINUTES

INGREDIENTS	CAL (KJ)
1 SMALL TEASPOON MISO PASTE	6 (25)
1 TEASPOON SOY SAUCE	5 (21)
1 CM (½ IN) PIECE OF GINGER, GRATED	2 (8)
1 TEASPOON LIME JUICE	2 (8)
½ BULB SPRING ONION (SCALLION), BULB AND STEM SLICED	2 (8)
15 G (½ OZ) WATERCRESS, WASHED	2 (8)
15 G (½ OZ) GREEN ASPARAGUS, PEELED AND CUT INTO SMALL PIECES	4 (17)
15 G (½ OZ) FRESH SHIITAKE MUSHROOMS, CLEANED	4 (17)
3 DROPS SESAME OIL	6 (25)
SALT AND PEPPER	
TOTAL	**33 (137)**

Preparing my soup

Combine the miso paste with 3 tablespoons of boiling water in a saucepan. Gradually add 250 ml (9 fl oz/1 cup) of boiling water, stirring. Add the soy sauce, ginger, lime juice, a very small amount of salt and some pepper, and bring to the boil. Simmer very gently for 5 minutes. Add the onion, watercress, asparagus and mushrooms. Pour into a bowl and sprinkle with sesame oil. Season with salt and pepper again, if necessary.

It's ready!

Extra: add 100 g (3½ oz) tofu (120 cal/502 kJ).

TOTAL 153 (639)

Tip: if you can't find fresh shiitake mushrooms, you can use dried ones instead. Weigh them after rehydrating them!

GREEN SOUP
& TOFU

113 *calories*

SERVES 1
PREPARATION TIME: 10 MINUTES
COOKING TIME: 22 MINUTES

INGREDIENTS	CAL (KJ)
50 G (1¾ OZ) SILVERBEET (SWISS CHARD) LEAVES, WASHED AND COARSELY CHOPPED	7 (29)
50 G (1¾ OZ) KALE LEAVES, WASHED AND COARSELY CHOPPED	25 (105)
1 CM (½ IN) PIECE OF GINGER, GRATED	2 (8)
½ GARLIC CLOVE, CHOPPED	2 (8)
50 G (1¾ OZ) TOFU, DICED	60 (251)
1 CORIANDER (CILANTRO) SPRIG, CHOPPED	1 (4)
1 FLAT-LEAF (ITALIAN) PARSLEY SPRIG, CHOPPED	1 (4)
½ TEASPOON SESAME SEEDS	13 (54)
¼ LIME	2 (8)
TOTAL	**113 (471)**

GLUTEN-FREE ◆

Preparing my soup

Heat the silverbeet and kale leaves in a medium saucepan for 2 minutes, stirring. Add the ginger, garlic, 200 ml (7 fl oz) of boiling water, salt and pepper. Let it cook for 10 minutes, then allow it to cool slightly before blending. Return the soup to the saucepan, add the tofu and cook for a further 10 minutes over a low heat. Pour into a bowl, add the chopped coriander and parsley, and sprinkle with the sesame seeds. Serve with the lime quarter to squeeze over the top.

It's ready!

Variation: replace the silverbeet with mâche lettuce (also known as corn salad or lamb's lettuce) (18 cal/75 kJ) and the kale with Chinese cabbage (wong bok) (6 cal/25 kJ).

TOTAL 105 (437)

Shopping: kale is a kind of curly-leafed cabbage, packed with vitamins! It's something you'll see more and more of in stores. Order it from your favourite greengrocer.

GAZPACHO

139 *calories*

SERVES 1
PREPARATION TIME: 15 MINUTES
REFRIGERATION TIME: 2 HOURS

INGREDIENTS	CAL (KJ)
2 TOMATOES, ABOUT 150 G (5½ OZ)	**27 (113)**
⅓ CUCUMBER, ABOUT 125 G (4½ OZ)	**15 (63)**
¼ GREEN CAPSICUM (PEPPER), ABOUT 50 G (1¾ OZ)	**17 (71)**
¼ RED CAPSICUM (PEPPER), ABOUT 50 G (1¾ OZ)	**17 (71)**
½ ONION, SLICED	**14 (59)**
½ GARLIC CLOVE, CHOPPED	**2 (8)**
1 TABLESPOON WINE VINEGAR	**2 (8)**
1 TEASPOON OLIVE OIL	**45 (188)**
TOTAL	**139 (581)**

GLUTEN-FREE ◆

Preparing my soup

Wash the vegetables. Chop the tomato, cucumber and capsicum (remove all of the seeds). Purée to a smooth soup with the onion, garlic, vinegar and olive oil. Season with salt and pepper. Refrigerate for at least 2 hours so it's well chilled. Serve with ice cubes.

It's ready!

Tip: you can pass the soup through a chinois or fine sieve before putting it in the refrigerator.

Variation: another version of gazpacho that's different and so good. The method is the same. It is best to pass the soup through a chinois or a fine sieve before serving.

⅓ CUCUMBER	**15 (63)**
¼ AVOCADO	**80 (335)**
½ GRANNY SMITH APPLE	**40 (167)**
1 BULB SPRING ONION (SCALLION)	**3 (13)**
JUICE OF ½ LIME	**4 (17)**
2 CORIANDER (CILANTRO) SPRIGS	**2 (8)**
1 BASIL SPRIG	**1 (4)**
1 PARSLEY SPRIG	**1 (4)**
1 CM (½ IN) PIECE OF GINGER	**2 (8)**
1 TEASPOON OLIVE OIL	**45 (188)**
TOTAL	**193 (807)**

TOMATO
& GOAT'S CHEESE SALAD

163 *calories*

SERVES 1

PREPARATION TIME: 10 MINUTES

INGREDIENTS	CAL (KJ)
250 G (9 OZ) FIRM SEASONAL TOMATOES, WASHED AND CUT INTO WEDGES	45 (188)
25 G (1 OZ) ASHED GOAT'S CHEESE	65 (272)
1 TEASPOON OLIVE OIL	45 (188)
1 TEASPOON BALSAMIC VINEGAR	5 (21)
2 CHIVES, SNIPPED	1 (4)
1 BASIL SPRIG, LEAVES PICKED	1 (4)
1 MINT SPRIG, LEAVES PICKED	1 (4)
TOTAL	163 (682)

GLUTEN-FREE ◆

Preparing my meal
Arrange the tomato wedges on a plate with the piece of goat's cheese. Drizzle with olive oil and balsamic vinegar, sprinkle with salt and give a turn of the pepper mill. Add the herbs and serve immediately.

It's ready!

My advice: this salad is excellent with seasonal tomatoes; choose them in a few different colours!

AL DENTE
QUINOA

150 calories

SERVES 1

COOKING TIME: 7 MINUTES

RESTING TIME: 5 MINUTES

INGREDIENTS	CAL (KJ)
40 G (1½ OZ) UNCOOKED QUINOA, WILL MAKE 85 G (3 OZ) COOKED	150 (628)
TOTAL	**150 (628)**

Rinse the quinoa and cook it in one and a half times its volume of boiling salted water for 7 minutes. Let the quinoa stand off the heat for 5 minutes. It should be perfectly cooked—light, crunchy, fluffy and delicious.

Variation: for a spiced version, add 1 pinch of cumin (1 cal/4 kJ), 1 pinch of saffron (1 cal/4 kJ) and ¼ preserved lemon (5 cal/21 kJ), chopped into small cubes, to the cooking water; don't add salt.

 Tip: I often cook two to three servings to keep in the refrigerator, where it will keep 3–6 days.

ONE PORTION
OF KIDNEY BEANS

SERVES 1

COOKING TIME: 1 HOUR 30 MINUTES MAXIMUM

SOAKING TIME: OVERNIGHT

INGREDIENTS	CAL (KJ)
45 G (1½ OZ) UNCOOKED KIDNEY BEANS, WILL MAKE 110 G (3¾ OZ) COOKED	150 (628)
TOTAL	**150 (628)**

Soak the beans in cold water overnight in the refrigerator. Rinse them, drain and place in a saucepan with three times their volume of cold water and start heating. Allow 1–1½ hours cooking time on a very low simmer, depending on how firm you want them to be. Season once they're cooked.

Variation: for a more flavoured version, add 1 clove (1 cal/4 kJ), ¼ onion, chopped (7 cal/29 kJ), 1 thyme sprig (1 cal/4 kJ) and 1 small bay leaf (1 cal/4 kJ) to the cooking water.

 Tip: I often cook two to three servings to keep in the refrigerator. They will keep for 1–3 days in the refrigerator, but you can also keep them in the freezer for several months.

PERFECT
WHOLE BLACK RICE

SERVES 1

COOKING TIME: 1 HOUR MAXIMUM

INGREDIENTS	CAL (KJ)
45 G (1½ OZ) UNCOOKED WHOLE BLACK RICE, WILL MAKE 90 G (3¼ OZ) COOKED	150 (628)
TOTAL	**150 (628)**

Place three parts cold water to one part rice in a small saucepan. Bring to the boil, add salt and allow 45 minutes to 1 hour cooking time over medium heat. The rice should open and show its pale interior, but if the grains are curved, it is already overcooked.

Variation: for a spicy version, add 1 small red chilli (1 cal/4 kJ) to the cooking water.

Tip: if you don't like whole black rice, replace it with 45 g (1½ oz) brown basmati rice (150 cal/628 kJ). White rice has a higher glycaemic index, so it should be consumed in moderation. Do try whole black rice though—it's so good. You will find it easily in organic food stores or online. To cook brown basmati rice, allow one part rice to three parts salted water. Start cooking in cold water and once it comes to the boil, count 35 minutes cooking time over medium heat.

Warning: don't keep cooked rice in the refrigerator for more than a day, as it could develop harmful bacteria.

MUSSEL
SALAD

262 calories

SERVES 1
PREPARATION TIME: 20 MINUTES
COOKING TIME: 10 MINUTES

INGREDIENTS	CAL (KJ)
300 G (10½ OZ) MUSSELS IN THEIR SHELLS, SCRUBBED AND DEBEARDED	128 (536)
1 SMALL FRENCH SHALLOT, CHOPPED	7 (29)
1 TABLESPOON WHITE WINE	8 (33)
1 TEASPOON OLIVE OIL	45 (188)
1 TEASPOON CIDER VINEGAR	2 (8)
75 G (2½ OZ) COOKED KIDNEY BEANS	67 (280)
1 BULB SPRING ONION (SCALLION), BULB AND STEM THINLY SLICED	3 (13)
3 FLAT-LEAF (ITALIAN) PARSLEY SPRIGS, CHOPPED	2 (8)
TOTAL	262 (1095)

GLUTEN-FREE ◆

Preparing my meal

Make sure the mussels are quite clean. Heat a large frying pan and add the mussels with the shallot, 50 ml (1½ fl oz) of water, the white wine, olive oil, salt and pepper. Cover and allow the shells to open. Shake the frying pan from time to time and allow 5 minutes cooking time so that all the shells are open. Drain the mussels, collecting the cooking juices. Strain the juice, add the cider vinegar and reduce by half over medium heat for 5 minutes. Rinse and drain the cooked kidney beans, and put them into a large bowl. Add the mussels, onion and parsley, and dress with the juices. Mix together, taste and adjust the salt and pepper if necessary.

It's ready!

Dried bean option: for this option, use 20 g (¾ oz) dried kidney beans. To cook the beans, follow the instructions on the packet before using (or see the recipe for kidney beans on page 124).

'Super 500' version: double the quantities, with the exception of the olive oil, to make a super easy 'Super 500' dish.

TOTAL 479 (2002)

'Super 500' variation for men: triple the quantity of kidney beans, and double the rest.

225 G (8 OZ) COOKED KIDNEY BEANS OR 60 G (2¼ OZ) DRIED	202 (845)
TOTAL	592 (2475)

FLASH-SEARED TUNA

180 calories

SERVES 1

PREPARATION TIME: 10 MINUTES

MARINATING TIME: 1 HOUR

COOKING TIME: 2 MINUTES

INGREDIENTS	CAL (KJ)
100 G (3½ OZ) RAW BLUEFIN TUNA, VERY FRESH	108 (452)
1 TEASPOON OLIVE OIL	45 (188)
1 TEASPOON SOY SAUCE	5 (21)
1 TEASPOON RICE VINEGAR	2 (8)
⅓ TEASPOON AGAVE SYRUP	8 (33)
25 G (1 OZ/1 HANDFUL) BABY ENGLISH SPINACH	6 (25)
20 G (¾ OZ) SPROUTS (SUCH AS CABBAGE OR ALFALFA)	6 (25)
TOTAL	**180 (752)**

Preparing my meal

Marinate the tuna in a mixture of the olive oil, soy sauce, rice vinegar, agave syrup and pepper. Refrigerate for 1 hour, turning the piece over from time to time. Wash the spinach and combine with the sprouts. Heat a frying pan over high heat and sear the tuna for 1 minute on each side: it needs to stay very red inside. Place the tuna on a plate, cover with spinach and sprouts, and pour over the rest of the marinade. Season with salt and pepper, if necessary.

It's ready!

 Tip: for something a little different, you can replace the baby English spinach with purslane (pigweed) or rocket—the calories are the same.

 Raw version: slice the tuna very thinly, sprinkle with the marinade, refrigerate for 1 hour, then serve with the mixed salad on top.

CEVICHE

191 calories

SERVES 1

PREPARATION TIME: 15 MINUTES

MARINATING TIME: 2 HOURS

INGREDIENTS	CAL (KJ)
¼ RED CHILLI	1 (4)
JUICE AND GRATED ZEST OF ½ UNTREATED (ORGANIC) LIME	5 (21)
3 CORIANDER (CILANTRO) SPRIGS, CHOPPED	2 (8)
1 FLAT-LEAF (ITALIAN) PARSLEY SPRIG, CHOPPED	1 (4)
1 BULB SPRING ONION (SCALLION), BULB AND STEM THINLY SLICED	3 (13)
100 G (3½ OZ) RAW SEA BASS FILLET, VERY FRESH (ALTERNATIVELY, USE OTHER FIRM WHITE FISH)	125 (523)
4 CHERRY TOMATOES, ABOUT 50 G (1¾ OZ)	9 (38)
1 TEASPOON OLIVE OIL	45 (188)
TOTAL	191 (799)

GLUTEN-FREE ◆

Preparing my meal

Finely chop the chilli and remove the seeds (don't put too much chilli in—it's better to add more later if needed!). Make the marinade with the lime juice and zest, half the chopped herbs, the onion and chilli. Clean and dry the fish and cut into small pieces. Put the pieces in a dish and pour over the marinade. Refrigerate for at least 2 hours (the longer the fish stays in the refrigerator, the more it will 'cook'). Wash the tomatoes, cut them in half, remove the soft pulp and chop the flesh into small pieces. Add the tomato pieces to the ceviche, season very lightly with salt and pepper, and scatter over the rest of the chopped herbs with a little olive oil. Serve immediately.

It's ready!

Variation: replace the sea bass with very fresh raw sea bream, cod or salmon.

100 G (3½ OZ) SEA BREAM	**100 (418)**	
TOTAL	**166 (694)**	
100 G (3½ OZ) COD	**80 (335)**	
TOTAL	**146 (611)**	
100 G (3½ OZ) SALMON	**166 (695)**	
TOTAL	**232 (971)**	

STEAMED FISH

& CRISP GREEN BEANS

SERVES 1

PREPARATION TIME: 20 MINUTES

COOKING TIME: 20 MINUTES

INGREDIENTS	CAL (KJ)
100 G (3½ OZ) GREEN BEANS, WASHED AND TRIMMED	31 (130)
1 SMALL FRENCH SHALLOT, FINELY CHOPPED	7 (29)
120 G (4¼ OZ) COD FILLET, OR OTHER FIRM WHITE FISH	96 (402)
4 CHERRY TOMATOES, ABOUT 50 G (1¾ OZ)	9 (38)
1 TEASPOON LEMON JUICE	2 (8)
2 BLACK OLIVES, PITTED	13 (54)
4 BASIL LEAVES	1 (4)
TOTAL	**159 (665)**

GLUTEN-FREE ◆

Preparing my meal

Put the green beans and shallot in a steamer basket, and steam for 20 minutes. After 10 minutes, add the fish fillet. Purée the tomatoes with the lemon juice, olives, basil, a little salt and pepper, and 2 tablespoons of water. Check to see if the fish is cooked (it should start to flake and be a pearly colour). Serve the fish and beans dressed with the sauce.

It's ready!

Variation: replace the cod with fillets of red mullet and place them on the green beans 5 minutes before the end of the cooking time.

120 G (4¼ OZ) RED MULLET (OR TRY SEA BASS OR OCEAN PERCH)	111 (464)
TOTAL	**174 (727)**

Extra: serve this dish with basmati rice (see page 124 for how to cook rice).

30 G (1 OZ) RAW BASMATI RICE	105 (439)
COD VERSION TOTAL	**264 (1104)**
RED MULLET VERSION TOTAL	**279 (1167)**

159 calories

SCALLOPS
& MUSHROOMS

156 *calories*

SERVES 1

PREPARATION TIME: 15 MINUTES

COOKING TIME: 15 MINUTES

INGREDIENTS	CAL (KJ)
4 SCALLOPS, ABOUT 120 G (4¼ OZ), CORAL (ROE) REMOVED	104 (435)
50 G (1¾ OZ) GIROLLE (CHANTERELLE) MUSHROOMS	10 (42)
1 SMALL FRENCH SHALLOT, CHOPPED	7 (29)
1 TARRAGON SPRIG, LEAVES PICKED	1 (4)
5 G (⅛ OZ) LIGHTLY SALTED BUTTER	34 (142)
FLEUR DE SEL (FINE SEA SALT)	
TOTAL	**156 (652)**

GLUTEN-FREE ◆

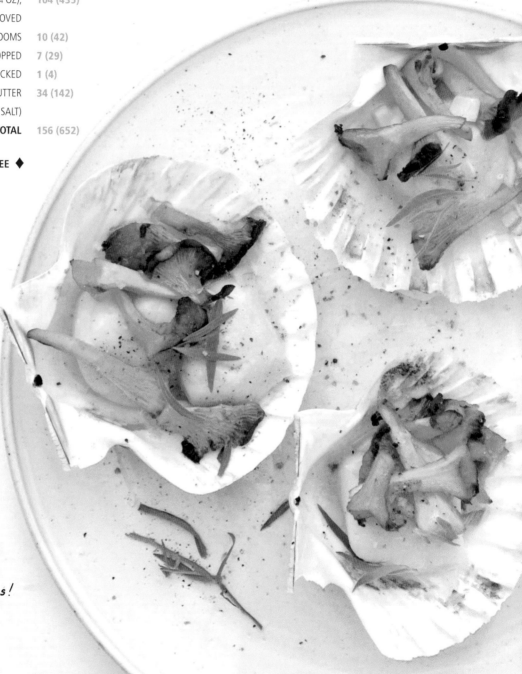

Preparing my meal

Ask the fishmonger to prepare the scallops: cleaned, coral removed, on their shells but detached. Arrange 2 scallops on each shell. Trim the mushroom stems and clean the mushrooms gently with a damp cloth. Cut the largest ones into a few pieces. Preheat the oven to 180°C (350°F). Divide the shallot and tarragon leaves among the shells. Add the mushrooms directly to the shells. Dot with small pieces of butter, sprinkle with sea salt and give a turn of the pepper mill. Bake for 15 minutes.

It's ready!

Extra: serve with a bowl of whole black rice (see page 124 for how to cook black rice).

45 G (1½ OZ) WHOLE BLACK RICE	150 (628)
TOTAL	**306 (1280)**

On a personal note: I love this recipe, with its mixture of briny and earthy flavours!

FISH TARTARE
& MANGO

179 *calories*

SERVES 1

PREPARATION TIME: 15 MINUTES

INGREDIENTS	CAL (KJ)
100 G (3½ OZ) RAW SEA BREAM, VERY FRESH	100 (418)
¼ MANGO, ABOUT 30 G (1 OZ)	20 (84)
1 CM (½ IN) PIECE OF GINGER, GRATED	2 (8)
5 CORIANDER (CILANTRO) SPRIGS, LEAVES CHOPPED	3 (13)
3 MINT LEAVES, CHOPPED	1 (4)
25 G (1 OZ/1 HANDFUL) BEAN SPROUTS	8 (33)
1 TEASPOON OLIVE OIL	45 (188)
FLEUR DE SEL (FINE SEA SALT)	
TOTAL	179 (748)

GLUTEN-FREE ◆

Preparing my meal

Dice the fish and mango and combine them in a bowl. Add the ginger, coriander and mint, and the bean sprouts, cut into short lengths. Dress with the olive oil, season lightly with sea salt and add some freshly ground black pepper. Mix together and refrigerate before serving.

It's ready!

Variation: replace the bream with very fresh salmon. It's also very good but has significantly more calories.

100 G (3½ OZ) RAW SALMON	166 (695)
TOTAL	245 (1025)

Tip: I recommend waiting a little while before eating the tartare—it tastes better.

Less sweet version: replace the mango with thinly sliced pink radishes.

30 G (1 OZ) PINK RADISH	6 (25)
TOTAL	165 (690)

ZUCCHINI
& PRAWNS

148 *calories*

SERVES 1

PREPARATION TIME: 10 MINUTES

MARINATING TIME: 30 MINUTES (OPTIONAL)

INGREDIENTS	CAL (KJ)
½ ZUCCHINI (COURGETTE), ABOUT 125 G (4½ OZ), THINLY SLICED	21 (88)
100 G (3½ OZ) COOKED PRAWNS (SHRIMP), PEELED	80 (335)
1 TARRAGON SPRIG, LEAVES PICKED	1 (4)
1 TEASPOON OLIVE OIL	45 (188)
GRATED ZEST OF ½ AN UNTREATED (ORGANIC) LIME	1 (4)
TOTAL	148 (619)

GLUTEN-FREE ◆

Preparing my meal

Put the zucchini slices and prawns in a bowl. Add the tarragon leaves, salt, pepper and olive oil. Mix and marinate in the refrigerator for 30 minutes before serving, if desired. Though the marinating time is optional, it tastes better if it has marinated for a while.

It's ready!

Variation: add some freshly grated parmesan cheese at the last minute.

10 G (¼ OZ) PARMESAN CHEESE	44 (184)
TOTAL	192 (803)

Extra nutritious variation: add some rocket, quinoa and chickpeas. (See page 124 for how to cook quinoa.)

25 G (1 OZ/1 HANDFUL) ROCKET (ARUGULA)	6 (25)
25 G (1 OZ) RAW QUINOA	92 (385)
30 G (1 OZ) COOKED CHICKPEAS	111 (464)
TOTAL	357 (1493)

FISH
WITH A THAI JUS

213 *calories*

INGREDIENTS	CAL (KJ)
1 SMALL FRENCH SHALLOT, CHOPPED	7 (29)
1 CM (½ IN) PIECE OF GINGER, GRATED	2 (8)
4 KAFFIR LIME LEAVES OR 1 LEMONGRASS STEM	2 (8)
½ GARLIC CLOVE	2 (8)
5 CORIANDER (CILANTRO) SPRIGS, CHOPPED	3 (13)
1 SMALL RED CHILLI	2 (8)
JUICE OF ½ LIME	4 (17)
25 G (1 OZ) RICE VERMICELLI	91 (381)
100 G (3½ OZ) COD FILLET, OR OTHER FIRM WHITE FISH	100 (418)
TOTAL	**213 (890)**

GLUTEN-FREE ◆

Preparing my meal

Make a stock with 750 ml (26 fl oz/3 cups) of water, the shallot, ginger, kaffir lime leaves or lemongrass cut into short lengths, the garlic, coriander, chilli, lime juice and salt. Cook on a gentle simmer for 30 minutes. Add the rice vermicelli and fish, and cook for 5 minutes over low heat. Place the vermicelli and fish in a deep plate, add a few tablespoons of broth and season lightly with salt and pepper.

It's ready!

Extra: for a more complete meal, add green beans, steamed for 10–15 minutes.

100 G (3½ OZ) GREEN BEANS	31 (130)
TOTAL	**244 (1020)**

GRILLED SQUID
WITH LEMON

157 *calories*

SERVES 1
PREPARATION TIME: 15 MINUTES
MARINATING TIME: 1 HOUR (OPTIONAL)
COOKING TIME: 2 MINUTES

INGREDIENTS	CAL (KJ)
100 G (3½ OZ) CLEANED SQUID TUBES	92 (385)
GRATED ZEST AND JUICE OF 1 UNTREATED (ORGANIC) LIME	10 (42)
1 TEASPOON OLIVE OIL	45 (188)
½ GARLIC CLOVE	2 (8)
FLEUR DE SEL (FINE SEA SALT)	
25 G (1 OZ/1 LARGE HANDFUL) ROCKET (ARUGULA)	6 (25)
2 BASIL SPRIGS, LEAVES PICKED	2 (8)
TOTAL	157 (656)

GLUTEN-FREE ◆

Preparing my meal

Slice the squid tubes into strips, chop the tentacles into small pieces, rinse and dry well. Marinate the squid pieces in a mixture of the lime juice, olive oil, garlic, a little sea salt and pepper. Place in the refrigerator for 1 hour, if desired. Combine the washed and dried rocket with the basil leaves. Drain the squid, but reserve the marinade. Heat a frying pan until very hot and sear the squid for 1 minute over high heat to brown well. Continue cooking for 1 minute, stirring constantly. Serve immediately with the salad dressed with the rest of the marinade. Finish by topping the squid with lime zest.

It's ready!

Tip: be careful when cooking the squid: the longer you cook it, the more rubbery it becomes. Make sure the frying pan is very hot so it sears rather than stews.

Extra: cook some pasta (such as spaghetti or penne) until *al dente*, refresh it under cold water, drain and toss with the salad while still warm. Yum, yum.

60 G (2¼ OZ) PASTA	207 (866)
TOTAL	364 (1522)

BLINIS
& SMOKED SALMON

284 *calories*

SERVES 1

PREPARATION TIME: 20 MINUTES

COOKING TIME: 1 MINUTE

INGREDIENTS	CAL (KJ)
2 TABLESPOONS (20 G/¾ OZ) OAT BRAN	49 (205)
1 TABLESPOON (10 G/¼ OZ) FROMAGE BLANC, 20% FAT (ALTERNATIVELY, USE QUARK OR YOGHURT CHEESE)	8 (33)
1 SMALL EGG	54 (226)
6 CHIVES, SNIPPED	2 (8)
2 DROPS OLIVE OIL	5 (21)
1 TABLESPOON (20 ML/½ FL OZ) SOY CREAM, WELL CHILLED	34 (142)
70 G (2½ OZ) SMOKED SALMON	126 (527)
GRATED ZEST OF ½ UNTREATED (ORGANIC) LEMON	6 (25)
TOTAL	**284 (1187)**

Preparing my meal

Combine the oat bran with the fromage blanc, add the egg and whisk together. Then add half the chives and a little salt and pepper. Add the olive oil to a frying pan and wipe it over the base with some paper towel—it's just so the blinis doesn't stick and browns a little. Heat the frying pan and pour in the batter, spreading it out to a pancake shape. Cook for 30 seconds on each side. Whisk the soy cream to make it more light and frothy. Lightly season with salt. Serve the blinis with the smoked salmon and cream, sprinkle with lemon zest, the rest of the chives and freshly ground black pepper.

It's ready!

Variation: replace the smoked salmon with salmon roe.

50 G (1¾ OZ) SALMON ROE	**126 (527)**
TOTAL	**284 (1187)**

Tip: if you don't like soy cream, you can use light crème fraîche (12% fat) instead—it has the same number of calories.

SEAFOOD
& BROTH

238 *calories*

SERVES 1
PREPARATION TIME: 20 MINUTES
COOKING TIME: 20 MINUTES

INGREDIENTS	CAL (KJ)
2–3 SCALLOPS, ABOUT 60 G (2½ OZ), CORAL (ROE) REMOVED	52 (218)
50 G (1¾ OZ) SMOKED MACKEREL, OR OTHER FATTY, FLAKY-TEXTURED FISH, SUCH AS TROUT	82 (343)
25 G (1 OZ) JERUSALEM ARTICHOKE	18 (75)
25 G (1 OZ) KOHLRABI	10 (42)
½ TEASPOON BLACK SESAME SEEDS	13 (54)
1 TEASPOON PUMPKIN SEED OIL	45 (188)
1 SMALL FRENCH SHALLOT, CHOPPED	7 (29)
1 CM (½ IN) PIECE OF GINGER, GRATED	2 (8)
4 KAFFIR LIME LEAVES OR 1 LEMONGRASS STEM, CUT INTO SECTIONS	2 (8)
½ GARLIC CLOVE	2 (8)
6 CORIANDER (CILANTRO) SPRIGS, LEAVES AND STEMS, CHOPPED	3 (13)
1 SMALL RED CHILLI	2 (8)
TOTAL	238 (994)

GLUTEN-FREE ◆

Preparing my meal

Clean the scallops and mackerel and chop them into small cubes (as for a tartare). Peel the Jerusalem artichoke and kohlrabi, and chop them into small cubes. Combine with the fish and scallops. Salt lightly, season with pepper, add the sesame seeds and pumpkin seed oil, combine and set aside in the refrigerator. In a medium saucepan make a broth with 500 ml (17 fl oz/ 2 cups) of water, the shallot, ginger, kaffir lime leaves or lemongrass stem, the garlic, half the coriander, the chilli and some salt. Cook on a gentle simmer for 20 minutes, then strain the broth. Taste the broth and adjust the salt and pepper if necessary. At serving time, pour the very hot broth over the fish and vegetable mixture, and scatter over the rest of the coriander.

It's ready!

My advice: if you can't find Jerusalem artichokes and kohlrabi, replace them with diced raw zucchini.

100 G (3½ OZ) ZUCCHINI (COURGETTE)	17 (71)
TOTAL	227 (948)

Shopping: you can find pumpkin seed oil in organic food stores or online. Alternatively, you can replace it with olive oil or hazelnut oil.

Variation: replace the smoked mackerel with a white fish such as smoked cod.

50 G (1¾ OZ) SMOKED COD	40 (167)
TOTAL	196 (818)

Extra: serve with a bowl of burghul.

20 G (¾ OZ) BURGHUL (BULGUR)	206 (862)
TOTAL	444 (1856)

OMELETTE
WITH HAM, TOMATO & SALAD

182 *calories*

SERVES 1
PREPARATION TIME: 20 MINUTES
COOKING TIME: 5 MINUTES

INGREDIENTS	CAL (KJ)
2 SMALL EGGS	**108 (452)**
½ TEASPOON OLIVE OIL	**23 (96)**
1 PINCH GROUND CUMIN	**1 (4)**
4 CHERRY TOMATOES, ABOUT 50 G (1¾ OZ), CUT INTO SMALL PIECES	**9 (38)**
25 G (1 OZ/1 SLICE) HAM, FAT REMOVED AND CHOPPED	**30 (126)**
25 G (1/OZ/1 HANDFUL) MIXED SALAD LEAVES	**6 (25)**
1 CHERVIL SPRIG, LEAVES PICKED	**1 (4)**
1–2 MUSHROOMS, ABOUT 15 G (½ OZ)	**4 (17)**
TOTAL	**182 (762)**

Preparing my meal

Beat the eggs with the olive oil, cumin, salt and pepper. Place a frying pan over high heat and pour in the eggs. Let the omelette set slightly for 1 minute, reduce the heat and top with the tomatoes and ham, then let it set for another 1–2 minutes. Fold over the omelette and transfer to a plate. Mix the salad leaves and chervil, and thinly slice the mushrooms (with a mandoline if you have one) at the last moment. Serve the omelette with the chervil salad and mushrooms on top. Season with salt and pepper.

It's ready!

Tip: beat the eggs for quite a while so that they become nice and foamy and the omelette is very light.

My advice: cep (porcini) mushrooms are a tasty alternative. If you're able to get fresh ones, make sure to remove any green foam from under the cep mushroom cap before slicing.

Indulgent variation: dollop some ricotta on the tomato and ham.

25 G (1 OZ) RICOTTA CHEESE	**35 (146)**
TOTAL	**217 (908)**

CHICKEN
BROCHETTES & LEMONGRASS

SERVES 1

PREPARATION TIME: 15 MINUTES

MARINATING TIME: 1 HOUR

COOKING TIME: 8 MINUTES

INGREDIENTS	CAL (KJ)
1 LEMONGRASS STEM	2 (8)
JUICE OF 1 LIME	8 (33)
1 TEASPOON OLIVE OIL	45 (188)
1 GARLIC CLOVE, CRUSHED	4 (17)
4 CORIANDER (CILANTRO) SPRIGS, CHOPPED	2 (8)
4 MINT LEAVES, CHOPPED	2 (8)
150 G (5½ OZ) CHICKEN BREAST FILLET	180 (753)
1 PINCH ESPELETTE PEPPER (PIMENT D'ESPELETTE)	1 (4)
ALTERNATIVELY, USE CHILLI POWDER	
OR CHILLI FLAKES	
TOTAL	244 (1019)

GLUTEN-FREE ◆

Preparing my meal

Remove the outer layer of the lemongrass stem and trim the base. Chop the more tender part, and stop as soon as it becomes woody. Purée the lemongrass, lime juice, olive oil, garlic, coriander and mint with 50 ml (1½ fl oz) of water and some pepper. Slice the chicken into roughly equal 3 cm (1¼ in) cubes. Thread them onto skewers. Marinate the chicken in the lemongrass mixture in the refrigerator for 1 hour. Heat a frying pan over medium heat and add the brochettes (set the marinade aside). Cook them for 2 minutes on each side, cover and cook them for a further 2 minutes over low–medium heat. Heat the marinade for 2 minutes before serving it with the brochettes sprinkled with Espelette pepper.

It's ready!

Extra: for a more substantial meal, serve with quinoa (see page 124 for how to cook quinoa) and rocket.

30 G (1 OZ) RAW QUINOA	110 (460)
25 G (1 OZ/1 HANDFUL) ROCKET (ARUGULA)	6 (25)
TOTAL	360 (1504)

244 *calories*

BEEF
MEATBALLS

246 *calories*

SERVES 1
PREPARATION TIME: 15 MINUTES
COOKING TIME: 25 MINUTES

INGREDIENTS	CAL (KJ)
2 MEDIUM TOMATOES, ABOUT 200 G (7 OZ)	36 (151)
⅓ TEASPOON GROUND CUMIN	2 (8)
1 SMALL RED CHILLI	2 (8)
G (5½ OZ) MINCED (GROUND) BEEF, 5% FAT	193 (808)
1 SMALL FRENCH SHALLOT, CHOPPED	7 (29)
1 CM (½ IN) PIECE OF GINGER, GRATED	2 (8)
5 CORIANDER (CILANTRO) SPRIGS, CHOPPED	2 (8)
5 MINT LEAVES, CHOPPED	2 (8)
TOTAL	**246 (1028)**

GLUTEN-FREE ◆

Preparing my meal
Purée the tomatoes with 100 ml (3½ fl oz) of water, salt, pepper and cumin. Put in a medium saucepan with the chilli over medium–high heat for 20 minutes. Meanwhile, combine the beef mince in a bowl with the shallot, ginger, coriander, mint and some pepper. Shape into meatballs the size of a large walnut. Brown the meatballs in a non-stick frying pan over high heat for 2 minutes, then add them to the sauce and continue cooking for 3 minutes. Remember to remove the chilli from the sauce before serving!

It's ready!

Extra: for a more balanced meal, serve with some kidney beans (see page 124 for cooking instructions) and baby English spinach.

	CAL (KJ)
25 G (1 OZ) DRIED KIDNEY BEANS	84 (351)
25 G (1 OZ) BABY ENGLISH SPINACH	6 (25)
TOTAL	**336 (1404)**

THAI TARTARE

211 *calories*

SERVES 1
PREPARATION TIME: 15 MINUTES

INGREDIENTS	CAL (KJ)
1 LEMONGRASS STEM	2 (8)
¼ RED CHILLI, SEEDS REMOVED AND FINELY CHOPPED	1 (4)
1 BULB SPRING ONION (SCALLION), BULB AND STEM CHOPPED	3 (13)
1 CM (½ IN) PIECE OF GINGER, PEELED AND CUT INTO MATCHSTICKS	2 (8)
3 CORIANDER (CILANTRO) SPRIGS, CHOPPED	2 (8)
100 G (3½ OZ) BEEF TENDERLOIN, CUT INTO SMALL CUBES	150 (628)
1 TEASPOON OLIVE OIL	45 (188)
½ TEASPOON FISH SAUCE	5 (21)
GRATED ZEST OF ½ UNTREATED (ORGANIC) LIME	1 (4)
TOTAL	**211 (882)**

Preparing my meal

Remove the outer layer of the lemongrass stem and trim the base. Chop the more tender part, and stop as soon as it becomes woody. Combine the prepared vegetables and herbs with the meat, pour over the olive oil and fish sauce, mix again and set aside in the refrigerator before serving. Sprinkle with the lime zest at serving time.

It's ready!

Tip: if you have a good butcher, simply get a piece of rump steak—it will be just as good, and have fewer calories.

100 G (3½ OZ) RUMP STEAK	136 (569)
TOTAL	**197 (823)**

Light version: serve with rocket.

25 G (1 OZ/1 HANDFUL) ROCKET (ARUGULA)	6 (25)
TOTAL	**217 (907)**

Extra: serve with a bowl of brown basmati rice (see page 124 for how to cook rice).

30 G (1 OZ) RAW BASMATI RICE	105 (439)
TOTAL	**316 (1321)**

ULTRA SPICY

BEEF SALAD

SERVES 1

PREPARATION TIME: 10 MINUTES

COOKING TIME: 1 MINUTE

INGREDIENTS	CAL (KJ)
5–10 DROPS TABASCO® SAUCE	1 (4)
½ BULB SPRING ONION (SCALLION), CHOPPED	2 (8)
2 CORIANDER (CILANTRO) SPRIGS, CHOPPED	2 (8)
1 PARSLEY SPRIG, FINELY CHOPPED	1 (4)
JUICE AND GRATED ZEST OF ½ UNTREATED (ORGANIC) LIME	5 (21)
2 TEASPOONS TOMATO SAUCE (KETCHUP)	10 (42)
½ GARLIC CLOVE, CRUSHED	2 (8)
1 TEASPOON OLIVE OIL	45 (188)
1 TEASPOON SWEET AND SOUR SAUCE	5 (21)
2 SUCRINE (OR BABY COS) LETTUCE HEARTS	15 (63)
100 G (3½ OZ) BEEF TENDERLOIN	150 (628)
½ TEASPOON SESAME SEEDS	13 (54)
TOTAL	**251 (1049)**

Preparing my meal

Make the sauce in a bowl by combining the Tabasco® sauce, onion, coriander, parsley, lime juice and zest, tomato sauce, garlic, olive oil and sweet and sour sauce. Mix well and set aside at room temperature. Wash the lettuce hearts and cut them into wedges. Sear the meat in a frying pan over high heat for 30 seconds on each side. Slice it thinly, place it on a plate and sprinkle with the sesame seeds. Add the lettuce, seasoned with salt and pepper, and serve with the ultra spicy sauce.

It's ready!

Tip: this dish is perfect to follow a 'light' aperitif between friends!

Warning: this dish is really very spicy and won't be to everyone's taste.

251 calories

SWEET & SAVOURY
WITLOF

154 calories

SERVES 1

PREPARATION TIME: 10 MINUTES

INGREDIENTS	CAL (KJ)
150 G (5½ OZ) WITLOF (CHICORY)	26 (109)
½ PEAR, ABOUT 90 G (3¼ OZ)	50 (209)
1 TEASPOON LEMON JUICE	2 (8)
25 G (1 OZ/1 SLICE) HAM, FAT REMOVED AND CUT INTO SMALL PIECES	30 (126)
1 TARRAGON SPRIG, LEAVES PICKED	1 (4)
1 TEASPOON WALNUT OIL	45 (188)
TOTAL	154 (644)

Preparing my meal

Discard the two or three outer leaves of the witlof. Trim the base and take out the central core at the bottom to remove the bitterness. Slice into strips. Peel the pear, remove the core, chop the pear into small pieces and sprinkle with the lemon juice. Put the witlof, pear and ham in a bowl, scatter over the tarragon leaves, dress with the walnut oil, and season with pepper and a little salt. Gently combine and serve immediately.

It's ready!

Tip: double the amount of ham for a meal that's still less than 200 calories (around 840 kilojoules).

TOTAL	184 (770)

Variation: finely grate some vieux (aged) Comté cheese over the salad at the last moment. Use a Microplane® grater—they're really handy!

10 G (¼ OZ) VIEUX (AGED) COMTÉ CHEESE	40 (167)
TOTAL	194 (811)

SEARED VEAL
& MUSHROOMS

259 calories

SERVES 1

PREPARATION TIME: 20 MINUTES

COOKING TIME: 5 MINUTES

INGREDIENTS	CAL (KJ)
120 G (4¼ OZ) VEAL TENDERLOIN	168 (703)
1 TEASPOON OLIVE OIL	45 (188)
1 HANDFUL (25 G/1 OZ) BABY SALAD LEAVES	6 (25)
200 G (7 OZ) SEASONAL MUSHROOMS	40 (167)
TOTAL	259 (1083)

GLUTEN-FREE ◆

Preparing my meal

Brush both sides of the meat with olive oil. Heat a frying pan and once it's very hot, sear the meat on one side. When the fillet has turned 'white' two-thirds of the way up, set it aside covered with foil. Wash the salad leaves and mushrooms (cut off any ends with soil on them and remove any other dirt with a damp cloth), and slice them into roughly equal pieces. Reheat the frying pan over high heat, add the mushrooms and cook for 2 minutes without stirring. Return the meat to the pan, uncooked side down, and cook for 1 minute. Then season with salt and pepper and serve. Place the salad leaves on top at the last minute.

It's ready!

Tip: you can also sear the meat in a hot frying pan without any oil and sprinkle the olive oil on the salad leaves.

On a personal note: I love this dish, which has the flavour of the forest. Feel free to use a combination of wild mushrooms and regular mushrooms. Count about 20 calories (84 kilojoules) per 100 g (3½ oz) mushrooms.

Chapter 3

NON-FAST DAY RECIPES

ENERGY
SOUP

SERVES 4

PREPARATION TIME: 15 MINUTES

INGREDIENTS

100 G (3½ OZ) ENGLISH SPINACH, WASHED

1 TEASPOON WAKAME SEAWEED POWDER

1 ZUCCHINI (COURGETTE), PEELED AND COARSELY CHOPPED

⅓ CUCUMBER, PEELED AND COARSELY CHOPPED

8 BASIL LEAVES

2 CM (¾ IN) PIECE OF GINGER, GRATED

2 TABLESPOONS SOY SAUCE

1 TABLESPOON ALMOND BUTTER

FLEUR DE SEL (FINE SEA SALT)

1 TEASPOON FLAXSEEDS

1 TEASPOON PEPITAS (PUMPKIN SEEDS)

1 TEASPOON MUSTARD SEED

Preparing my soup

Put into the bowl of a mixer or a blender: the spinach leaves, seaweed powder, zucchini, cucumber, basil, ginger, soy sauce, almond butter, 250 ml (9 fl oz/1 cup) of water, a very small amount of fine sea salt and a little freshly ground pepper. Process, taste, add a little more water if necessary. Combine the flaxseeds, pepitas and mustard seeds in a small bowl. Serve the soup, sprinkled with the seeds.

It's ready!

Tip: this soup is very energising and very good cold, but on winter evenings, you can heat it up very gently in a saucepan.

GREEN
GAZPACHO

SERVES 4

PREPARATION TIME: 15 MINUTES

INGREDIENTS

2 CUCUMBERS AND 2 ZUCCHINI (COURGETTES), PEELED

2 BULB SPRING ONIONS (SCALLIONS)

½ GREEN CAPSICUM (PEPPER)

JUICE OF 2 LIMES

2 CM (¾ IN) PIECE OF GINGER, GRATED

2 TEASPOONS PEPITAS (PUMPKIN SEEDS)

2 TEASPOONS LINSEEDS (FLAXSEEDS)

2 TEASPOONS BROWN MUSTARD SEEDS

1 AVOCADO

1 TABLESPOON CANOLA OIL

FLEUR DE SEL (FINE SEA SALT)

Preparing my soup

Process the cucumbers, zucchini, onions and capsicum with 300 ml (10½ fl oz) of water, the lime juice and ginger until smooth. Strain if necessary and add a little water, if needed. Set aside in the refrigerator. Mix the seeds together. Dice the avocado and serve in individual bowls with the soup. At the last moment add a drizzle of canola oil, the sea salt, freshly ground pepper and seeds on top.

It's ready!

Extra: for a more complete meal, add 50 g (1¾ oz) of diced very fresh raw salmon.

QUICK PISTOU
SOUP

NON-
FAST
Day

SERVES 4

PREPARATION TIME: 25 MINUTES

COOKING TIME: 20 MINUTES

INGREDIENTS

1 CELERY STALK, CHOPPED

150 G (5½ OZ) GREEN BEANS, TRIMMED AND CUT INTO SHORT LENGTHS

1 LARGE POTATO (SKIN ON IF ORGANIC), CUT INTO LARGE CUBES

100 G (3½ OZ/⅔ CUP) SHELLED PEAS

1 LITRE (35 FL OZ/4 CUPS) HOT CHICKEN STOCK

1 FIRM ZUCCHINI (COURGETTE) (SKIN ON IF ORGANIC), CUT INTO LARGE CUBES

200 G (7 OZ) COOKED WHITE BEANS

10 CHERRY TOMATOES, HALVED

60 G (2¼ OZ/½ BUNCH) BASIL

½ GARLIC CLOVE

25 G (1 OZ) PINE NUTS

25 G (1 OZ/¼ CUP) GRATED PARMESAN CHEESE

2½ TABLESPOONS OLIVE OIL

Preparing my soup

Put the celery, green beans, potato, peas and stock into a heavy stockpot. Cover and simmer very gently for 15 minutes. Add the zucchini, white beans and tomato, and cook for a further 5 minutes. Make the pesto by processing the basil leaves with the garlic, pine nuts, parmesan cheese, a little salt, pepper and the olive oil. Serve the soup very hot with 1 tablespoon pesto in each bowl.

It's ready!

On a personal note: I'm not a big fan of garlic, so I only put in half a clove, but you can always add more to taste.

PROSCIUTTO
& BEAN SALAD

Non-Fast Day

SERVES 4

PREPARATION TIME: 20 MINUTES

COOKING TIME: 15 MINUTES

INGREDIENTS

250 G (9 OZ) GREEN BEANS

25 G (1 OZ) PINE NUTS, TOASTED

2 BULB SPRING ONIONS (SCALLIONS), BULBS AND STEMS SLICED

8 SLICES PROSCIUTTO, CUT INTO PIECES

40 G (1½ OZ/½ BUNCH) CORIANDER (CILANTRO), CHOPPED

50 G (1¾ OZ/2 HANDFULS) MIXED SALAD LEAVES

1 SMALL TABLESPOON MAPLE SYRUP

2 TABLESPOONS OLIVE OIL

FLEUR DE SEL (FINE SEA SALT)

60 G (2¼ OZ) AGED MIMOLETTE CHEESE

(ALTERNATIVELY, USE PARMESAN CHEESE)

Preparing my meal

Steam the green beans for 15 minutes: they should remain tender-crisp. Run them under cold water to cool them down and stop them cooking any further. Drain and place them in a salad bowl. Add the pine nuts, onions, prosciutto, coriander and mixed salad leaves. Make the dressing by mixing the maple syrup with the olive oil, a little sea salt and some freshly ground black pepper. At the last minute, dress the salad and finish with shavings of mimolette (or parmesan), made with a vegetable peeler.

It's ready!

 Extra: for a more complete meal, add one soft-boiled egg per person to the salad. Cooking time: 5–6 minutes, then peel under cold running water.

Variation: replace the prosciutto with bresaola (alternatively, use beef jerky or other dried meat).

PUMPKIN SOUP
À L'ORANGE

SERVES 4
PREPARATION TIME: 15 MINUTES
COOKING TIME: 25 MINUTES

INGREDIENTS

1 SMALL HOKKAIDO PUMPKIN (SQUASH),
ABOUT 1.2 KG (2 LB 10 OZ)
JUICE AND GRATED ZEST OF 1 UNTREATED
(ORGANIC) ORANGE
1 BOUQUET GARNI: PARSLEY, THYME, BAY LEAF
FLEUR DE SEL (FINE SEA SALT)
FEW DROPS OLIVE OIL

GLUTEN-FREE ◆

Preparing my soup

Wash and scrub the skin of the pumpkin (if it's organic, leave the skin on—otherwise peel). Cut into large cubes. Remove the seeds and put all of the pieces into a large saucepan with the orange juice and zest, the bouquet garni and a little sea salt and freshly ground pepper. Cover with water and cook until the pieces are tender, about 25 minutes. Remove the pumpkin from the broth, but reserve the liquid. Purée the pumpkin with a little broth and gradually thin it out, ladleful by ladleful with the broth, until it's the consistency you like. Taste and adjust the seasoning and serve immediately, sprinkled with a few drops of olive oil.

It's ready!

On a personal note: I love drinking this soup when it's cold outside. I add chopped toasted hazelnuts and 2–3 tablespoons wild rice.

FENNEL
& WITLOF SALAD

Non-Fast Day

SERVES 4

PREPARATION TIME: 20 MINUTES

INGREDIENTS

2 WITLOF (CHICORIES)

2 SMALL FENNEL BULBS

½ PRESERVED LEMON

20 CAPERBERRIES, RINSED

6 FLAT-LEAF (ITALIAN) PARSLEY SPRIGS, CHOPPED

JUICE OF ½ LEMON

½ TEASPOON MUSTARD

½ TEASPOON CRÈME FRAÎCHE

½ TABLESPOON WHITE WINE VINEGAR

2 TABLESPOONS OLIVE OIL

2 TABLESPOONS CRUSHED ALMONDS

Preparing my meal

Discard the two or three outer leaves of the witlof. Don't wash them. Trim the bases and cut out the central core at the bottom to remove the bitterness. Slice into strips. Remove the hard outer layer of the fennel bulbs. Thinly slice the fennel using a good knife or a mandoline. Wash the slices under water and drain. Rinse the preserved lemon under water and cut it into small pieces (remove the seeds). Combine the fennel, witlof, preserved lemon, caperberries and parsley. Make the dressing: mix together the lemon juice, mustard, crème fraîche, white wine vinegar, olive oil and a little freshly ground pepper. Pour over, then toss the salad to combine and keep in the refrigerator before serving. Serve with the crushed almonds scattered on top.

It's ready!

Extra: for a more substantial salad, add 150 g (5½ oz) drained and flaked tuna at the last moment.

ZUCCHINI
& PARMESAN

NON-FAST Day

SERVES 4

PREPARATION TIME: 15 MINUTES

INGREDIENTS

1 TABLESPOON OLIVE OIL

1 TEASPOON PUMPKIN SEED OIL

1 TEASPOON HAZELNUT OIL

2 YELLOW ZUCCHINI (COURGETTES)

(OR 4 IF THEY ARE REALLY SMALL)

2 MINT SPRIGS, LEAVES PICKED

1 TABLESPOON TOASTED, CRUSHED HAZELNUTS

50 G (1¾ OZ) PARMESAN CHEESE

GLUTEN-FREE ◆

Preparing my meal

Make the vinaigrette by combining the oils with a little sea salt and freshly ground pepper. Pour the sauce over the base of a large plate (where you'll lay out the zucchini when it's sliced). Wash and scrub the zucchini and slice them very thinly using a mandoline or a very sharp knife. Spread them out on the plate and top with the mint leaves and hazelnuts. Grate the parmesan over the top and serve immediately.

It's ready!

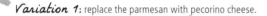

Variation 1: replace the parmesan with pecorino cheese.

Variation 2: you can replace the pumpkin seed oil and hazelnut oil with just olive oil. Use about 2 tablespoons in total.

Extra: for a substantial salad to have for lunch, I add mozzarella and thin slices of finely shredded prosciutto.

Shopping: you can find pumpkin seed oil in organic food stores or online.

SWEET SALAD

Non-Fast Day

SERVES 4

PREPARATION TIME: 20 MINUTES

INGREDIENTS

2 CM (¾ IN) PIECE OF GINGER, GRATED

1 FRENCH SHALLOT, CHOPPED

1 TABLESPOON RICE VINEGAR

1 TABLESPOON VEGETABLE OIL

½ TEASPOON SOY SAUCE

½ TEASPOON FISH SAUCE

JUICE OF ½ LIME

1 MANGO, RIPE BUT STILL FAIRLY FIRM, PEELED AND DICED

300 G (10½ OZ) CARROTS, GRATED

30 G (1 OZ/2 LARGE HANDFULS) CORIANDER

(CILANTRO) LEAVES, CHOPPED

10 MINT LEAVES

Preparing my meal

Make the dressing: mix together the ginger, shallot, rice vinegar, vegetable oil, soy sauce, fish sauce, lime juice and pepper. Mix together the mango, carrots and herbs and add the dressing. Taste and adjust the salt and pepper if necessary.

It's ready!

ASPARAGUS,

ZUCCHINI & FETA SALAD

SERVES 4

PREPARATION TIME: 15 MINUTES

COOKING TIME: 10 MINUTES

INGREDIENTS

400 G (14 OZ) GREEN ASPARAGUS,
BASE ENDS TRIMMED

205 G (7¼ OZ/1⅓ CUPS) SHELLED PEAS

2 SMALL FIRM ZUCCHINI (COURGETTES),
SLICED INTO THIN ROUNDS

100 G (3½ OZ/⅔ CUP) CRUMBLED FETA CHEESE

25 G (1 OZ/1 LARGE HANDFUL) ROCKET (ARUGULA)

1 TABLESPOON TOASTED SESAME SEEDS

GRATED ZEST OF 1 UNTREATED (ORGANIC) LEMON

1–2 TABLESPOONS OLIVE OIL

GLUTEN-FREE ◆

Non-Fast Day

Preparing my meal

Cook the asparagus and peas in salted boiling water for 10 minutes, then place in a bowl of ice-cold water to stop them cooking any further. Drain and dry on paper towel. Combine the asparagus, peas, zucchini, feta, rocket, sesame seeds and lemon zest in a bowl or on a serving plate. Sprinkle with the olive oil, season with salt and pepper, and serve immediately.

It's ready!

Extra: add chicken breasts, browned in a frying pan. First, marinate them in 1 tablespoon olive oil, 2 tablespoons lemon juice, 1 tablespoon agave syrup and ½ teaspoon ground cumin. Cook for 3 minutes on each side over high heat, then over low heat for 3 minutes.

SPICY CHICKPEA
SALAD

Non-
Fast
Day

SERVES 4

PREPARATION TIME: 20 MINUTES

COOKING TIME: 2 MINUTES

INGREDIENTS

60 G (2¼ OZ) CHORIZO, THINLY SLICED

2 TEASPOONS WHITE WINE VINEGAR

1 TEASPOON HOT MUSTARD

2 TABLESPOONS OLIVE OIL

FLEUR DE SEL (FINE SEA SALT)

400 G (14 OZ) COOKED CHICKPEAS

1 AVOCADO, DICED

2 BULB SPRING ONIONS (SCALLIONS),
BULBS AND STEMS THINLY SLICED

5 FLAT-LEAF (ITALIAN) PARSLEY SPRIGS

2 TARRAGON SPRIGS

GRATED ZEST OF 1 UNTREATED (ORGANIC) LIME

Preparing my meal

Put the chorizo slivers into a medium frying pan over medium heat and brown them on both sides for 1–2 minutes. Drain them on paper towel. In a salad bowl, make a dressing from the white wine vinegar, mustard, olive oil, a little sea salt and lots of freshly ground pepper. Add the chickpeas, avocado, onions, parsley, tarragon and chorizo. Mix together well and sprinkle with the lime zest.

It's ready!

SUPER
TABOULEH

SERVES 4
PREPARATION TIME: 25 MINUTES
COOKING TIME: 10 MINUTES
REFRIGERATION TIME: 3 HOURS

Non-Fast Day

INGREDIENTS
JUICE OF 1 LEMON
1 TABLESPOON CANOLA OIL
1 TABLESPOON HAZELNUT OIL
FLEUR DE SEL (FINE SEA SALT)
200 G (7 OZ) GREEN ASPARAGUS
½ CAULIFLOWER
1 SMALL CUCUMBER
8 CHERRY TOMATOES
2 BULB SPRING ONIONS (SCALLIONS)
60 G (2¼ OZ) SEMI-WHOLEGRAIN COUSCOUS
4 MINT SPRIGS, CHOPPED
4 FLAT-LEAF (ITALIAN) PARSLEY SPRIGS, CHOPPED

Preparing my meal

In a large bowl, combine the lemon juice with the oils, a little sea salt and two or three turns of the pepper mill. Prepare the asparagus: trim the bases, then peel the spears without touching the tips. Rinse them under cold water and steam them for around 10 minutes. Check whether they're ready with the tip of a knife: they should still be a little firm. Let them cool on paper towel. Wash the cauliflower and only keep the small florets (cut off all the stems). Using a mandoline, grate the florets to make little grains of cauliflower, and set these aside. Wash the cucumber, remove the seeds, and cut it into small cubes. Wash the tomatoes and cut them into wedges. Chop the onions and cut the asparagus into short lengths. Add all the ingredients to the dressing in the bowl: the cauliflower, cucumber cubes, onion, tomato, asparagus, couscous and chopped herbs. Mix together well and refrigerate for at least 3 hours, stirring occasionally. Before serving, taste and adjust the seasoning.

It's ready!

Tip: to stop the herbs from being 'cooked' by the dressing (because of the lemon juice), you can also chop and mix them in at the last minute before serving.

WARM LENTIL SALAD

& HEIRLOOM VEGETABLES

NON-
FAST
Day

SERVES 4

PREPARATION TIME: 20 MINUTES

COOKING TIME: 32 MINUTES

INGREDIENTS

150 G (5½ OZ/⅔ CUP) LENTILS

50 G (1¾ OZ) SMOKED BACON, CHOPPED

1 SMALL PARSNIP, CUT INTO STICKS

150 G (5½ OZ) BUTTERNUT PUMPKIN (SQUASH)

PEELED, SEEDED AND CUT INTO SMALL CUBES

1 TABLESPOON LINSEEDS (FLAXSEEDS)

25 G (1 OZ) SUNFLOWER SEEDS, TOASTED

25 G (1 OZ) PINE NUTS, TOASTED

1 TABLESPOON BALSAMIC GLAZE

2 TABLESPOONS ORANGE JUICE

2 TABLESPOONS OLIVE OIL

FLEUR DE SEL (FINE SEA SALT)

Preparing my meal

In a saucepan, cover the lentils with water and cook for 25 minutes in total, including the time they take to come to the boil. The lentils should be *al dente*. Set aside. Drop the bacon into boiling water for 1 minute, drain and place on paper towel. Heat a large frying pan and add the chopped bacon. Add the parsnip and pumpkin and brown over high heat for 2–3 minutes. Stir with a wooden spoon, reduce the heat slightly and cook for 3–4 minutes. Roughly crush the seeds (linseeds, sunflower seeds) and pine nuts. To make the vinaigrette: mix the balsamic glaze, orange juice and olive oil, and season with sea salt and freshly ground pepper. Combine the lentils with the parsnip, pumpkin and seed and nut mixture; add the dressing, taste and adjust the seasoning.

It's ready!

Extra: cook two duck breasts in a hot frying pan, 7 minutes on the skin side and 3 minutes on the flesh side. Drain, allow to cool until just warm, and slice thinly before serving with the salad.

Classic version: replace the parsnip with carrots and use pumpkin (winter squash) instead of butternut.

CREAM OF LENTIL SOUP
WITH HADDOCK

NON-FAST Day

SERVES 4

PREPARATION TIME: 20 MINUTES

SOAKING TIME: OVERNIGHT

COOKING TIME: 30 MINUTES

INGREDIENTS

200 G (7 OZ) SMOKED HADDOCK

1 LITRE (35 FL OZ/4 CUPS) MILK

200 G (7 OZ) TINY BLUE-GREEN LENTILS

2 FRENCH SHALLOTS, CHOPPED

½ LEEK, PALE PART ONLY, CHOPPED

1 SMALL CARROT, CHOPPED

100 ML (3½ FL OZ) THIN (POURING) CREAM

50 ML (1½ FL OZ) WHITE WINE

300 ML (10½ FL OZ) HOT CHICKEN STOCK

1 TABLESPOON SESAME SEEDS, TOASTED

Preparing my soup

Soak the haddock for several hours or overnight in the milk. In a large saucepan, cook the lentils with the shallots, leek and carrot in a large quantity of water seasoned with salt and pepper for 30 minutes. Put the vegetables and cooking liquid through a food mill. Transfer the mixture to a blender and add the cream and white wine. Blend, check the texture and gradually add the stock, little by little, until the soup is the consistency you want. Add a little pepper if necessary, but don't add salt because the haddock is already salty enough. Reheat very gently in a saucepan before serving. Drain the haddock, wipe it dry and cut it into small cubes (without the skin). Serve the soup nice and hot with the cubes of haddock on top and sprinkled with sesame seeds.

It's ready!

On a personal note: I really like the consistency of this soup when it's thick, and I enjoy it as a main course on chilly winter evenings.

Variation: replace the haddock with very fresh raw salmon.

SMOKED MACKEREL
& ROASTED BUCKWHEAT

NON-FAST Day

SERVES 4
PREPARATION TIME: 20 MINUTES
COOKING TIME: 7 MINUTES

INGREDIENTS

300 G (10½ OZ) ROASTED BUCKWHEAT (KASHA)

1 TABLESPOON CANOLA OIL

JUICE OF ½ LIME

FLEUR DE SEL (FINE SEA SALT)

300 G (10½ OZ) BUTTERNUT PUMPKIN (SQUASH)

2 TABLESPOONS OLIVE OIL

4 SMOKED MACKEREL FILLETS WITH CRUSHED
PEPPERCORNS, SKIN REMOVED AND FLAKED

25 G (1 OZ/1 HANDFUL) BABY ENGLISH SPINACH

4 CHERVIL SPRIGS, CHOPPED

GLUTEN-FREE ◆

Preparing my meal

Pour the buckwheat into a medium saucepan of boiling water and cook for 3–4 minutes. Taste: it should stay a little crunchy. Drain and pour the buckwheat into a salad bowl, dress with the canola oil and lime juice and season with sea salt and pepper. Remove the skin from the pumpkin and cut the flesh into small cubes. Heat a few drops of olive oil in a frying pan, add the cubes of pumpkin and brown over high heat for 2–3 minutes. Add the pumpkin to the bowl along with the mackerel, baby spinach and chervil. Dress with the remaining olive oil and a little sea salt, stir, taste and adjust seasoning if necessary.

It's ready!

Tip: you can warm up the mackerel for a few seconds before serving … it tastes even better!

Shopping: you can find smoked mackerel with crushed peppercorns in the refrigerated section of some organic stores or online. If you need a substitute, try another fatty, flaky-textured fish, such as herring or trout.

POT LUCK SALAD
WITH SMOKED MACKEREL

Non-Fast Day

SERVES 4

PREPARATION TIME: 20 MINUTES

COOKING TIME: 1½ HOURS

INGREDIENTS

100 G (3½ OZ/½ CUP) WHOLE BLACK RICE

100 G (3½ OZ) KIDNEY BEANS

1 SMALL FIRM ZUCCHINI (COURGETTE), DICED

1 SMALL ONION, SLICED

GRATED ZEST OF 1 UNTREATED (ORGANIC) LIME

200 G (7 OZ) CHERRY TOMATOES, QUARTERED

1 LEBANESE (SHORT) CUCUMBER, PEELED AND CUBED

1 AVOCADO, COARSELY CHOPPED

1 TABLESPOON MIXED SEEDS (SUNFLOWER, SESAME …)

A FEW TARRAGON LEAVES

1 TABLESPOON OLIVE OIL

1 TABLESPOON PUMPKIN SEED OIL

1 TABLESPOON WHITE OR DARK BALSAMIC GLAZE

4 SMOKED MACKEREL FILLETS WITH CRUSHED PEPPERCORNS

(OR OTHER FATTY, FLAKY-TEXTURED FISH SUCH AS TROUT)

GLUTEN-FREE ◆

Preparing my meal

Cook the black rice (see page 124) and kidney beans (see page 124). Put the rice and beans in a large mixing bowl and allow to cool. Add the zucchini, onion, lime zest, tomato, cucumber, avocado, seeds and tarragon leaves. Make the dressing with the olive oil, pumpkin seed oil, balsamic glaze, salt and a little pepper. Pour over the vegetables and mix together. Remove the skin from the mackerel fillets and serve with the salad.

It's ready!

Tip: add any seasonal vegetables to this salad, chopped into small pieces, even raw (Jerusalem artichokes, radish, carrots, celery, turnips, asparagus, mushrooms …).

My advice: if you don't like whole black rice, replace it with basmati rice (its glycaemic index is higher … but it is also very good!).

Shopping: you can find pumpkin seed oil, seeds and mackerel fillets in organic food stores or online.

On a personal note: ever since I discovered the mackerel fillets in the refrigerated aisle of my organic food store, I've been buying them all the time. You can warm them up for a few seconds in a saucepan of hot water, still in their packaging. They taste even better that way! I often cook my grains, beans and quinoa in large quantities that I keep in a pretty covered ceramic dish in the refrigerator for several days.

FISH
TARTARE

NON-
FAST
Day

SERVES 4

PREPARATION TIME: 20 MINUTES

COOKING TIME: 20 MINUTES

INGREDIENTS

80 G (2¾ OZ) TINY BLUE-GREEN LENTILS

400 G (14 OZ) RAW POLLACK, VERY FRESH

(ALTERNATIVELY, USE COD OR JOHN DORY)

1 BULB SPRING ONION (SCALLION),

BULB AND STEM THINLY SLICED

20 G (¾ OZ) FIRM CHORIZO, DICED

25 G (1 OZ/1 LARGE HANDFUL) ROCKET (ARUGULA)

2 TARRAGON SPRIGS, LEAVES PICKED

2 TABLESPOONS OLIVE OIL

FLEUR DE SEL (FINE SEA SALT)

Preparing my meal

Rinse the lentils, put them in a medium saucepan and cook them for 20 minutes in three times their volume of water over medium heat. Drain and allow to cool. Clean the pieces of fish, wipe them dry and cut into small cubes. Combine the fish with the onion, chorizo, rocket, lentils and tarragon leaves. Dress with the olive oil and sprinkle lightly with sea salt. Mix together and serve at room temperature or refrigerate to eat cold a little later.

It's ready!

Tip: serve this dish as a main meal—it's quite substantial!

Variation: replace the chorizo with 4 slices of prosciutto or bresaola.

SALMON
CHIRASHI
REVISITED

Non-
Fast
Day

SERVES 4

PREPARATION TIME: 20 MINUTES

COOKING TIME: 20 MINUTES

INGREDIENTS

150 G (5½ OZ) SUSHI RICE

2 TABLESPOONS RICE VINEGAR

230 G (8¼ OZ) RAW SALMON, VERY FRESH

FLEUR DE SEL (FINE SEA SALT)

1 AVOCADO

JUICE OF ½ LIME

1 CM (½ IN) PIECE OF GINGER, CHOPPED

1 TABLESPOON SOY SAUCE

1 TABLESPOON OLIVE OIL

1 TEASPOON SESAME OIL

1 TEASPOON BLACK SESAME SEEDS

8 CORIANDER (CILANTRO) SPRIGS, CHOPPED

Preparing my meal

Cook the rice following the instructions on the packet, drain, sprinkle with the rice vinegar and allow to cool. Rinse the salmon, pat dry and cut into small cubes. Season the salmon with sea salt and freshly ground pepper and set aside. Thinly slice the avocado and sprinkle with the lime juice so it doesn't oxidise. Make the dressing with the ginger, soy sauce, olive oil, sesame oil and a little pepper. Place the rice in the bottom of four serving dishes, top with the avocado, then the salmon. Dress with the sauce and sprinkle with sesame seeds and coriander.

It's ready!

Extra: replace the sushi rice with a glutinous rice to serve hot as a side to the salmon, with avocado served as a salad. Wash the rice until the water runs clear. Cover with water and soak for 12 hours (overnight) in the refrigerator. Drain and steam for 1 hour. The rice is cooked when it's translucent and perfectly sticky.

Variation: you can replace the salmon with very fresh raw sea bream or tuna, or large cooked prawns (shrimp).

Shopping: you can find black sesame seeds in organic food stores; alternatively, use standard sesame seeds, lightly toasted in a frying pan.

FISH
& PEAS

NON-FAST Day

SERVES 4

PREPARATION TIME: 10 MINUTES

COOKING TIME: 23 MINUTES

INGREDIENTS

400 G (14 OZ) SHELLED PEAS,

OR 1 KG (2 LB 4 OZ) IN THEIR PODS

8 CHERRY TOMATOES

60 G (2¼ OZ) CHORIZO, CHOPPED INTO SMALL CUBES

2 FRENCH SHALLOTS, CHOPPED

4 SEA BREAM FILLETS, OR OTHER FIRM WHITE FISH

3 BASIL SPRIGS, LEAVES PICKED

FLEUR DE SEL (FINE SEA SALT)

Preparing my meal

Steam the peas and tomatoes for 10 minutes. Sauté the chorizo cubes with the shallots in a frying pan over medium heat for 3 minutes. Drain on paper towel. Leave the frying pan on the heat and add the fish fillets to the pan. Cook over medium heat for 2 minutes each side, then over low heat for 2 minutes on each side with the pan covered. Add the peas and tomatoes, the chorizo and shallots and cook for a further 2 minutes over low heat. Check that the fish is cooked and serve immediately with the basil scattered over. Season with a little sea salt and freshly ground pepper as required.

It's ready!

Extra: serve with semi-wholegrain couscous. Allow 50 g (1¾ oz) per person. Pour one part boiling salted water (with two or three drops of olive oil) on one part couscous. Let it stand, covered, for 7 minutes, then fluff up with a fork.

GRILLED FISH
& VEGETABLE MASH

NON-FAST Day

SERVES 4
PREPARATION TIME: 20 MINUTES
COOKING TIME: 25 MINUTES

INGREDIENTS

8 BABY RED MULLET FILLETS
(ALTERNATIVELY, USE SEA BASS OR OCEAN PERCH)
400 G (14 OZ) POTATOES
2 ZUCCHINI (COURGETTES)
1 TEASPOON OLIVE OIL
50 G (1¾ OZ) SEMI-DRIED TOMATOES, CHOPPED
4 BASIL SPRIGS, CHOPPED
20 G (¾ OZ) PARMESAN CHEESE SHAVINGS
A FEW MINT LEAVES
FLEUR DE SEL (FINE SEA SALT)

GLUTEN-FREE ◆

Preparing my meal

Ask the fishmonger to prepare the red mullet fillets and make sure all the bones are removed. Wash and peel the vegetables (you can leave the skin on organic zucchini). Cut the vegetables into chunks and steam them for 20 minutes. Put them in a bowl with the olive oil, season with salt and pepper and crush them all together to make a lovely mash. Keep some solid pieces or not, according to taste. Mix in the semi-dried tomatoes and basil. Rinse and wipe dry the mullet fillets. Place a large sheet of baking paper in a heavy frying pan (or on a hotplate!). Add a drop of olive oil and once the pan is quite hot, lay down the fillets skin side down (in batches if necessary) and let them sear for 2–3 minutes. Reduce the heat, cover and cook for a further 2 minutes. Serve immediately with the mash, parmesan, mint, sea salt and pepper.

It's ready!

THE CLUB SANDWICH

SERVES 4

PREPARATION TIME: 10 MINUTES

INGREDIENTS

1 SMALL AVOCADO

JUICE OF ½ LIME

8 SLICES WHOLEMEAL BREAD, CRUSTS REMOVED

10 CHIVES, SNIPPED

10 CORIANDER (CILANTRO) SPRIGS, COARSELY CHOPPED

150 G (5½ OZ) TOMATOES, SLICED INTO ROUNDS

150 G (5½ OZ) CHICKEN BREAST FILLET, COOKED AND THINLY SLICED

4 LETTUCE LEAVES

Preparing my meal

Mash the avocado flesh with the lime juice, and season with salt and pepper. Toast the bread. Spread the mashed avocado on all the slices. Divide the herbs between four of the slices, then the tomato and chicken, and finish with a lettuce leaf. Place the remaining four slices of bread on top. Using a sharp knife, trim off any filling that's poking out the side and cut each sandwich in two for easier eating.

It's ready!

BEEF CARPACCIO

NON-FAST Day

SERVES 4

PREPARATION TIME: 20 MINUTES

FREEZING TIME: 2 HOURS

INGREDIENTS

400 G (14 OZ) BEEF TENDERLOIN OR HEART OF RUMP

½ FENNEL BULB

10 SMALL MUSHROOMS

4 ASPARAGUS SPEARS

2 BULB SPRING ONIONS (SCALLIONS)

25 G (1 OZ/1 LARGE HANDFUL) ROCKET (ARUGULA)

8 BLACK OLIVES, PITTED

2½ TABLESPOONS OLIVE OIL

FLEUR DE SEL (FINE SEA SALT)

GLUTEN-FREE ◆

Preparing my meal

Wrap the piece of beef in plastic wrap and place in the freezer for 2 hours. Wash the fennel bulb and remove the tough outer layer. Slice the bulb thinly, preferably with a mandoline. Clean the mushrooms with a damp cloth. Peel and chop the asparagus into rounds, and set aside the tips. Slice the onions thinly from top to bottom. Rinse and dry the rocket. Put the asparagus tips and pitted olives in the bowl of a food processor, add the olive oil, a little salt and pepper, and pulse the mixture a few times. Set aside. Take the piece of beef out of the freezer, remove the plastic wrap and slice the beef very thinly using a very sharp knife. Lay the slices on four chilled plates as you go. Dress with the sauce and garnish with the fennel, asparagus and onions. At the last minute, thinly slice the mushrooms over each plate using a mandoline, and add the rocket.

It's ready!

Extra: serve with black rice (see recipe page 124) and a little mozzarella.

Special treat variation: serve with a portion of oven-baked fries (fewer calories) or home-made mashed potato (use potatoes that have boiled or steamed for 20 minutes, then mash them with a fork with a little butter, olive oil, salt and pepper).

On a personal note: it's not essential to have all the vegetables. I use what I have in my refrigerator, and sometimes I even ask my butcher to slice some carpaccio directly onto my plates! I also often add some parmesan cheese. It's so good, but I grate it very finely, which means I use less.

THE SUNDAY ROAST
CHICKEN

Non-Fast Day

SERVES 4

PREPARATION TIME: 10 MINUTES

COOKING TIME: 1½ HOURS

INGREDIENTS

1 FREE-RANGE CHICKEN, ABOUT 1.5 KG (3 LB 5 OZ)

1 TUB (30 G/1 OZ) PETIT-SUISSE CHEESE

(ALTERNATIVELY, USE RICOTTA)

3 CM (1¼ IN) PIECE OF GINGER, SLICED

1 UNTREATED (ORGANIC) LEMON, HALVED

OLIVE OIL

15 G (½ OZ) BUTTER

1 ONION, SLICED

1 VINE BRANCH OF CHERRY TOMATOES, PICKED

GLUTEN-FREE ◆

Preparing my meal

Preheat the oven to 200°C (400°F). Season the inside of the chicken with salt and pepper and empty the tub of petit-suisse inside the cavity with the sliced ginger and half the lemon (chopped). Put the chicken in a baking dish, coat it with olive oil and dot with pieces of the butter. Put the chicken in the oven. Baste regularly with its juices. After 45 minutes, arrange the onion, tomatoes and the rest of the lemon (chopped) around the chicken. Cook for another 45 minutes.

It's ready!

My advice: enjoy a beautiful chicken breast with the onions, tomatoes and lemon, but leave the fatty juices and chips to the others. Serve with a lovely green salad with herbs.

POT-AU-FEU

NON-FAST Day

SERVES 4

PREPARATION TIME: 20 MINUTES

COOKING TIME: 3½ HOURS

INGREDIENTS

700 G (1 LB 9 OZ) BRAISING BEEF (CHUCK, BLADE, SHIN, SHANK), FAIRLY LEAN

3 CARROTS, SLICED INTO 4 LENGTHWAYS

2 FRENCH SHALLOTS, PEELED

1 GARLIC CLOVE, PEELED

3 CM (1¼ IN) PIECE OF GINGER, THINLY SLICED

1 SMALL RED CHILLI

6 KAFFIR LIME LEAVES (OR LEMONGRASS STEMS)

1 TABLESPOON SOY SAUCE

1 TEASPOON PEPPERCORNS

1 TEASPOON COARSE SALT

8 CORIANDER (CILANTRO) SPRIGS, LEAVES AND STEMS CHOPPED

4 THAI EGGPLANT (AUBERGINE) OR 1 MEDIUM EGGPLANT, CUT INTO CHUNKS

1 HANDFUL BEAN SPROUTS

1 MINT SPRIG, LEAVES PICKED

1 LIME

Preparing my meal

Rinse the meat under cold water. Submerge it in a large flameproof casserole dish full of water and bring to the boil on the stovetop. Skim for as long as necessary, then remove the meat and rinse it. Preheat the oven to 140°C (275°F). Return the meat to the casserole dish, add the carrots, shallots, garlic, ginger, chilli, lime leaves (replace with 2 lemongrass stems if necessary, cut into short lengths), soy sauce, peppercorns, coarse salt and coriander (leaves and stems). Add enough water to just cover the meat and bring to the boil. Cover with the lid and cook in the oven for 2 hours. Wash the eggplant and the bean sprouts. Add the eggplant to the casserole dish and cook for a further 45 minutes. Add the bean sprouts and cook for a further 15 minutes. Serve the beef very hot, garnished with mint leaves and accompanied by the vegetables and broth. Add a little lime wedge to each plate.

It's ready!

Extra: for the bun bo version, add rice vermicelli to the broth 5 minutes before the end of the cooking time.

Tip: I love making this pot-au-feu ahead of time for nights when it's very cold outside. When there's leftover broth, I use it for a Fast Day with a big handful of bean sprouts, a few grated vegetables and 50 g (1¾ oz) beef tenderloin, chopped up tartare-style.

THAI-STYLE
PORK

NON-
FAST
Day

SERVES 4

PREPARATION TIME: 25 MINUTES

COOKING TIME: 2½ HOURS

REFRIGERATION TIME: A FEW HOURS
OR OVERNIGHT (OPTIONAL)

INGREDIENTS

800 G (1 LB 12 OZ) PORK SCOTCH (NECK) FILLET,
CUT IN PIECES

4 KAFFIR LIME LEAVES

30 G (1 OZ/2 LARGE HANDFULS) CORIANDER
(CILANTRO) LEAVES, CHOPPED

2 MINT SPRIGS, CHOPPED

1 GARLIC CLOVE, PEELED

3 FRENCH SHALLOTS, CUT INTO WEDGES

1 SMALL RED CHILLI

3 CM (1¼ IN) PIECE OF GINGER, GRATED

1 TABLESPOON SOY SAUCE

250 G (9 OZ/1¼ CUPS) BROWN JASMINE RICE

2 FENNEL BULBS

150 ML (5 FL OZ) COCONUT MILK

1 TEASPOON OLIVE OIL

Preparing my meal

Put the pork in a flameproof casserole dish with the kaffir lime leaves, half the coriander, half the mint, the garlic, shallots, chilli, ginger and soy sauce. Cover with water just to the top of the meat and bring to the boil on the stovetop. Preheat the oven to 180°C (350°F). Cover the casserole dish and bake in the oven for 2 hours. Set the meat aside and save the cooking broth. Cook the rice according to the instructions on the packet. Trim and wash the fennel bulbs, remove the hard outer layer, cut the bulbs into thick wedges and steam them for 15 minutes. Add the coconut milk to the broth once the fat has been skimmed (if you want to remove the fat beforehand, see tip below). Boil for 10 minutes, then add the meat and reheat very gently. Place the fennel wedges in a large ovenproof dish, sprinkle over the olive oil, stir and place under a grill (broiler) for 5–10 minutes so they're well browned. Remove the meat from the broth and serve in deep plates. Scatter the rest of the coriander and the fresh mint over the meat and rice. Serve the pork accompanied by the rice mixed with the fennel, and the broth on the side.

It's ready!

Tip: if you have time, make this dish the day before so you can skim the fat. It's better for your figure after all! In that case, take the meat out and leave it in a large dish in the refrigerator. Refrigerate the broth overnight or for a few hours so you can skim it more easily (remove the layer of fat that will form on top).

PUMPKIN, LAMB

& CHICKPEA TAGINE

NON-FAST Day

SERVES 4

PREPARATION TIME: 25 MINUTES

COOKING TIME: 2¼ HOURS

INGREDIENTS

800 G (1 LB 12 OZ) LAMB SHOULDER,
CUT INTO LARGE PIECES

1 TABLESPOON OLIVE OIL

2 ONIONS, SLICED

2 CM (¾ IN) PIECE OF GINGER, GRATED

1 GARLIC CLOVE, CHOPPED

1 PRESERVED LEMON, SEEDED AND CHOPPED
INTO SMALL PIECES

FLEUR DE SEL (FINE SEA SALT)

1 PINCH SAFFRON

500 ML (17 FL OZ/2 CUPS) CHICKEN STOCK

½ HOKKAIDO PUMPKIN (SQUASH)

200 G (7 OZ) COOKED CHICKPEAS

2 TABLESPOONS TOASTED, CRUSHED HAZELNUTS

2 MINT SPRIGS, LEAVES PICKED

Preparing my meal

Brown the meat with half the olive oil in a flameproof casserole dish on the stovetop. Do this in several batches if necessary. The dish should be very hot and the meat mustn't stew. Remove the meat, add the onions and sauté them with the remaining olive oil for 3 minutes over high heat. Lower the heat, add the ginger, garlic and preserved lemon, a little sea salt and some pepper. Blend the saffron into the stock and add it to the dish. Bring to the boil, return the meat to the dish, reduce the heat to the lowest setting, cover and cook for 2 hours. Meanwhile, wash the pumpkin, remove the skin if it is not organic, and cut the flesh into cubes. Add the pumpkin cubes 20 minutes before the end of the cooking time and the cooked chickpeas 10 minutes before the end. Check throughout the cooking time that there's enough liquid in the dish and add a little water if necessary. Check that the vegetables are cooked (cook for a few more minutes if necessary). Serve sprinkled with the hazelnuts and mint.

It's ready!

Extra: serve with semi-wholegrain couscous. Allow 50 g (1¾ oz) per person. Pour one part boiling salted water (with two or three drops of olive oil) on one part couscous. Let it stand, covered, for 7 minutes, then fluff up with a fork.

THAI DUCK BREAST
& CELLOPHANE NOODLES

NON-FAST Day

SERVES 4

PREPARATION TIME: 15 MINUTES

MARINATING TIME: 1 HOUR

COOKING TIME: 12 MINUTES

INGREDIENTS

2 TABLESPOONS SOY SAUCE

2 TABLESPOONS RICE VINEGAR

GRATED ZEST AND JUICE OF 1 UNTREATED

(ORGANIC) LIME

2 CM (¾ IN) PIECE OF GINGER, CUT INTO

THIN MATCHSTICKS

2 DUCK BREASTS

150 G (5½ OZ) CELLOPHANE NOODLES

2 BULB SPRING ONIONS (SCALLIONS),

BULBS AND STEMS THINLY SLICED

30 G (1 OZ/2 LARGE HANDFULS) CORIANDER

(CILANTRO) LEAVES, CHOPPED

1 TABLESPOON PEANUTS, CHOPPED

Preparing my meal

Make a marinade with the soy sauce, rice vinegar, the lime zest and juice and the ginger matchsticks. Season lightly with pepper. Score the duck skin and pour over the marinade. Refrigerate for 1 hour, turning the breasts from time to time. Preheat the oven to 240°C (475°F). Drain the duck breasts and cook them (skin side up) for 10 minutes in a baking dish. Keep them warm wrapped in foil and discard the fatty pan juices. Cook the noodles, following the instructions on the packet. Heat the marinade for 2 minutes, then combine with the noodles and onions. Serve the sliced duck garnished with coriander and peanuts, and accompanied by the noodles.

It's ready!

Tip: for breasts that are less pink, increase the cooking time by 3 minutes so they're more well done.

On a personal note: I cook the duck on a rack with a dish underneath to catch the fat and I throw it away. That way, my duck breasts aren't swimming in fat!

GRILLED CHICKEN
& CRUNCHY SALAD

NON-FAST Day

SERVES 4

PREPARATION TIME: 25 MINUTES

COOKING TIME: 11 MINUTES

MARINATING TIME: 1 HOUR

INGREDIENTS

3 TABLESPOONS OLIVE OIL

1 TABLESPOON MAPLE SYRUP

1 PINCH CHILLI POWDER

4 CHICKEN BREASTS, ABOUT 120 G (4¼ OZ) EACH

1 AVOCADO

JUICE OF ½ LEMON

80 G (2¾ OZ) BABY ENGLISH SPINACH

⅓ BLACK RADISH, ALTERNATIVELY USE TURNIP

OR SWEDE (RUTABAGA)

2 COOKED ARTICHOKE HEARTS, CUT INTO SMALL PIECES

1 TABLESPOON SESAME OIL

1 TABLESPOON MIRIN

1 TEASPOON SOY SAUCE

1 TEASPOON RICE VINEGAR

1 SMALL RED CHILLI, SEEDED AND CHOPPED

1 TEASPOON NIGELLA SEEDS

Preparing my meal

To make the marinade, mix 2 tablespoons of the olive oil, the maple syrup and chilli powder. Put the chicken breasts in the marinade and leave them in the refrigerator for 1 hour. Thinly slice the avocado and sprinkle it with the lemon juice so it doesn't oxidise. Rinse and dry the baby spinach, and peel and thinly slice the radish into slivers (this is very easy using a mandoline). Place all the vegetables in a mixing bowl and set aside. Heat a frying pan and sear the chicken breasts for 3 minutes over high heat, cover the pan, reduce the heat and continue cooking gently for 5 minutes. Let the chicken breasts cool until lukewarm and slice them thinly. Make the sauce by combining the sesame oil, the remaining olive oil, the mirin, soy sauce, rice vinegar, chilli, and a little salt and pepper. Pour the sauce over the salad, toss and serve with the chicken slices sprinkled with nigella seeds.

It's ready!

Shopping: buy nigella seeds in organic food stores. If you can't find them, you can replace them with sesame and/or sunflower seeds.

Variation: replace the chicken with salmon fillets, marinate them and cook in a hot frying pan for 2 minutes on each side. Wrap them in plastic wrap and refrigerate so they slice more easily, or serve as a whole fillet warm or even hot.

Warning: this is quite a spicy recipe. Go easy on the chilli if you have a low tolerance!

VEAL TENDERLOIN
& LOTS OF GRILLED VEGETABLES

NON-FAST Day

SERVES 4

PREPARATION TIME: 20 MINUTES

COOKING TIME: 1 HOUR

INGREDIENTS

200 G (7 OZ) EARLY OR NEW POTATOES

1 FIRM ZUCCHINI (COURGETTE)

1 SMALL BEETROOT (BEET)

4 SMALL TURNIPS

1 FENNEL BULB

½ PRESERVED LEMON

2 CM (¾ IN) PIECE OF GINGER, GRATED

2 TEASPOONS OLIVE OIL, PLUS EXTRA FOR DRIZZLING

5 G (⅛ OZ) BUTTER

480 G (1 LB 1 OZ) VEAL TENDERLOIN CUT INTO 8 PIECES

3 CHERVIL SPRIGS, CHOPPED

GLUTEN-FREE ◆

Preparing my meal

Preheat the oven to 210°C (410°F). Wash the vegetables and peel them if they're not organic—otherwise, leave the skin on. Remove the fennel's tough outer layer. Cut up the vegetables (the fennel into wedges, the potatoes, zucchini and beetroot into large cubes, the turnips in half). Finely chop the preserved lemon (remove the seeds). Place all the vegetables in a large dish with the ginger and preserved lemon, drizzle with the extra olive oil and season with salt and pepper. Bake for 1 hour, turning occasionally. For extra browning, place the vegetables under a grill (broiler) for 2–3 minutes before the end of the cooking time. Just before serving, heat the butter and 2 teaspoons of olive oil in a large frying pan. As soon as it's quite hot, add the pieces of veal. Wait until the pieces of meat turn white two-thirds of the way up, then baste them with the melted butter. Turn off the heat, turn over the pieces of meat and wait 3 minutes before serving with the vegetables. Sprinkle with chopped chervil and season the meat with salt and pepper at the table.

It's ready!

Light tip: you can also cook the meat without the oil and butter!

EXPRESS
JUICE!

MAKES 4 GLASSES
PREPARATION TIME: 5 MINUTES

INGREDIENTS
4 ORANGES
8 CARROTS, WELL WASHED
(OR ORGANIC CARROTS)
4 CM (1½ IN) PIECE OF GINGER

GLUTEN-FREE ◆

Making my drink
Peel the oranges and remove the seeds. Cut the carrots into
pieces and put all the ingredients through the juicer.

Drink immediately.

GREEN
SMOOTHIE

MAKES 4 GLASSES
PREPARATION TIME: 5 MINUTES

INGREDIENTS
½ CUCUMBER, PEELED
JUICE OF ½ LIME
150 ML (5 FL OZ) GRAPEFRUIT JUICE
(1 PINK GRAPEFRUIT)
1 AVOCADO
50 G (1¾ OZ/2 LARGE HANDFULS) ROCKET
(ARUGULA)
2 MINT SPRIGS, LEAVES PICKED
200 ML (7 FL OZ) COCONUT WATER
100 ML (3½ FL OZ) WATER

GLUTEN-FREE ◆

Making my drink
Process all the ingredients together in a blender, or a food processor
if you don't have a blender. Extend with a few ice cubes if necessary.

Drink immediately.

Indexes

MENU PLANS

RECIPE GUIDE

INDEX BY
INGREDIENT

4 WEEKS
OF MENU PLANS

Week
1
(Spring / Summer)

Monday Fast Day	Tuesday Non-Fast Day	Wednesday Non-Fast Day	Thursday Fast Day	Friday Non-Fast Day	Saturday Non-Fast Day	Sunday Non-Fast Day
	Breakfast	Breakfast		Breakfast	Breakfast	Brunch:
	◆ Thai tartare (p144) ◆ Black rice (p124) ◆ Steamed broccoli & soy sauce (p110)	◆ Pot luck salad with smoked mackerel (p170)		◆ Dip & crudités (p114) ◆ Omelette with ham, tomato & salad (p140)	◆ Spicy chickpea salad (p162) ◆ Green salad with herbs (p111) ◆ Cheese	◆ Express juice! (p198) ◆ The club sandwich (p180)
◆ Black rice, peas, asparagus & mint (p64)			◆ Pasta salad (p78)			
	◆ Grilled chicken & crunchy salad (p194) ◆ Quinoa (p124)	◆ Beef carpaccio (p182) ◆ Crisp & tangy salad (p102)		◆ Miso soup revisited (p120) ◆ Fish tartare (p172) ◆ Red rice ◆ 2 glasses of wine	◆ Grilled fish & vegetable mash (p178) ◆ Dessert ◆ 2 glasses of wine	◆ Thai duck breast & cellophane noodles (p192) ◆ Dessert ◆ 2 glasses of wine

Week
2
(Spring / Summer)

Monday Fast Day	Tuesday Non-Fast Day	Wednesday Non-Fast Day	Thursday Fast Day	Friday Non-Fast Day	Saturday Non-Fast Day	Sunday Non-Fast Day
	Breakfast	Breakfast		Breakfast	Breakfast	Brunch:
	◆ Salmon chirashi revisited (p174)	◆ Spring asparagus (p104) ◆ Tomato tart (p100)		◆ Chicken brochettes & lemongrass (p142) ◆ Grilled green beans (p113)	◆ Asparagus, zucchini & feta salad (p161) ◆ Super tabouleh (p163)	◆ Green smoothie (p198) ◆ Omelette with ham, tomato & salad (p140)
◆ Quinoa, tomatoes, preserved lemon & fresh herbs (p38)			◆ Al dente vegetables & eggs (p36)			
	◆ Steamed fish & crisp green beans (p130)	◆ Fennel & witlof salad (p158) ◆ Beef meatballs (p143)		◆ Creamy gazpacho (p152) ◆ Zucchini & prawns (p132) ◆ 2 glasses of wine	◆ Ultra spicy beef salad (p145) ◆ Black rice (p124) ◆ Dessert ◆ 2 glasses of wine	◆ Thai-style pork (p188) ◆ Dessert ◆ 2 glasses of wine

Week 1
(Autumn / Winter)

Monday Fast Day	Tuesday Non-Fast Day	Wednesday Non-Fast Day	Thursday Fast Day	Friday Non-Fast Day	Saturday Non-Fast Day	Sunday Non-Fast Day
	Breakfast	Breakfast		Breakfast	Breakfast	Brunch: • Express juice! (p198) • Blinis & smoked salmon (p136)
	• Seafood & broth (p138) • Black rice (p124)	• Miso soup (p120) • Grilled squid with lemon (p135) • Black rice (p124)	• Fish & vegetable curry (p74)	• Fish with a Thai jus (p134) • Black rice (p124)	• Omelette with ham, tomato & salad (p140) • Bread	
• Winter soup (p52)	• Pumpkin soup à l'orange (p157) • Bowl of pasta (p108)	• Warm lentil salad & heirloom vegetables (p164) • Zucchini & parmesan (p159)		• Pumpkin, lamb & chickpea tagine (p190) • 2 glasses of wine	• Fruity grated carrots (p103) • Cream of lentil soup (p166) • Dessert • 2 glasses of wine	• The Sunday roast chicken (p184) • Steamed heirloom vegetables (p106) • Dessert • 2 glasses of wine

Week 2
(Autumn / Winter)

Monday Fast Day	Tuesday Non-Fast Day	Wednesday Non-Fast Day	Thursday Fast Day	Friday Non-Fast Day	Saturday Non-Fast Day	Sunday Non-Fast Day
	Breakfast	Breakfast		Breakfast	Breakfast	Brunch: • The club sandwich (p180) • Express juice! (p198)
	• Seafood & broth (p138) • Quinoa (p124)	• Energy soup (p152) • Blinis & smoked salmon (p136)	• Pasta & vegetables (p48)	• Steamed fish & crisp green beans (p130) • Black rice (p124)	• Bowl of pasta (p108)	
• Like a chilli (p86)	• Veal tenderloin & lots of grilled vegetables (p196) • Black rice (p124)	• Prosciutto & bean salad (p156) • Beef meatballs (p143)		• Smoked mackerel & roasted buckwheat (p168) • 2 glasses of wine	• Fish & peas (p176) • Quinoa (p124) • Dessert • 2 glasses of wine	• Pot-au-feu (p186) & rice vermicelli • Dessert • 2 glasses of wine

RECIPE
GUIDE

Chapter 3
NON-FAST DAY RECIPES

INDEX BY INGREDIENT

ACKNOWLEDGMENTS

Delphine and Charlotte would like to thank:

Charlotte, 'the food photographer', for her talent, eye, style and good humour no matter what happens.

Marie-Pierre, 'the portrait photographer', for her lovely photo of the two of us, in which she captured the rapport that unites us on this wonderful project.

Chloé, who helped us during every session in the kitchen, for her energy and efficiency.

Raphaëlle, for her help in choosing the styling, tableware and backdrops, and for her availability.

Olivia, for all of the illustrations, the layout, the cover…we fell in love with your style, we adore it, we 100% approve!

And thanks of course to all the tasters, who followed 'our' 5:2 diet and tested the 'Super 500' recipes…so thank you to Grita, Sabine, Séverine, Alexandra, Isabella, Delphine and Julie!

Delphine would like to thank…Charlotte, my co-author, who I met at a nutrition/sophro/yoga workshop and who I immediately warmed to. Some time later she came to see me with this great project. I dived in, explored 5:2 in depth, we talked about it for hours and hours, made it completely our own and it has become more than a diet for me, but a genuine way of life.

Published in 2015 by Murdoch Books, an imprint of Allen & Unwin
First published by Marabout in 2014

Murdoch Books Australia
83 Alexander Street
Crows Nest NSW 2065
Phone: +61 (0) 2 8425 0100
Fax: +61 (0) 2 9906 2218
www.murdochbooks.com.au
info@murdochbooks.com.au

Murdoch Books UK
Erico House, 6th Floor
93–99 Upper Richmond Road
Putney, London SW15 2TG
Phone: +44 (0) 20 8785 5995
www.murdochbooks.co.uk
info@murdochbooks.co.uk

For Corporate Orders & Custom Publishing contact Noel Hammond,
National Business Development Manager, Murdoch Books Australia

Publisher: Corinne Roberts
Food Photographer: Charlotte Lascève
Portrait Photographer: Marie-Pierre Morel
Design: Transparence and Olivia Deslandes
Stylist: Raphaëlle Esneault
Translator: Melissa McMahon
Editor: Susie Ashworth
Editorial Manager: Barbara McClenahan
Production Manager: Mary Bjelobrk

Text and design copyright © Hachette Livre (Marabout) 2014

A cataloguing-in-publication entry is available from the catalogue
of the National Library of Australia at www.nla.gov.au.

ISBN 978 1 74336 547 2 Australia
ISBN 978 1 74336 532 8 UK

A catalogue record for this book is available from the British Library.

Colour reproduction by Splitting Image Colour Studio Pty Ltd, Clayton, Victoria
Printed by 1010 Printing International Limited, China

IMPORTANT: If you are under medical care for any condition or are taking medication of any description, please consult your doctor or health practitioner before acting on any suggestions in this book or before embarking on any fast. Neither the authors nor the publisher may be held responsible for claims resulting from information in this book.

Those who might be at risk from the effects of salmonella poisoning (the elderly, pregnant women, young children and those suffering from immune deficiency diseases) should consult their doctor with any concerns about eating raw eggs. Please ensure that all seafood and beef to be eaten raw or lightly cooked are very fresh and of the highest quality.

OVEN GUIDE: You may find cooking times vary depending on the oven you are using. For fan-forced ovens, as a general rule, set the oven temperature to 20°C (35°F) lower than indicated in the recipe.

MEASURES GUIDE: We have used 15 ml (3 teaspoon) tablespoon measures for recipes in this book.